MORE THAN
HALF WAY
HOME

TO TERRY
ROBERTA
FROM BOB &
KAREN KLEIN

Bob

The world needs dreamers like
you!

MORE THAN
HALF WAY
HOME

A Story of Accompaniment in
the Shadows of Incarceration

DUSTIN FEDDON

ORBIS BOOKS
Maryknoll, New York 10545

Published by Orbis Books, Box 302, Maryknoll, NY 10545-0302.

Note: Some names and details have been changed to protect privacy.

This is a work of nonfiction and is based on the author's memories of events, interactions, and research. While all efforts were made for accuracy, memory is subjective. Dialogues have been reconstructed and may not be verbatim. The events and perspectives presented reflect the author's recollections, which may differ from others who experienced the same events.

Manufactured in the United States of America

Library of Congress Cataloging-in-Publication Data

Names: Feddon, Dustin author
Title: More than half way home : a story of accompaniment in the shadows
  of incarceration / Dustin Feddon.
Description: Maryknoll, NY : Orbis Books, [2025] | Includes biographical
  references. | Includes bibliographical references. | Summary: "A priest's
  journey from ministering death row inmates to founding a community
  restoring dignity to the formerly incarcerated"—Provided by publisher.
Identifiers: LCCN 2025015744 (print) | LCCN 2025015745 (ebook) |
  ISBN 9781626986275 trade paperback | ISBN 9798888660829 epub
Subjects: LCSH: Church work with prisoners—Catholic Church | Church work
  with prisoners—United States | Feddon, Dustin
Classification: LCC BV4340 .F44 2025 (print) | LCC BV4340 (ebook) |
  DDC 259/.5—dc23/eng/20250609
LC record available at https://lccn.loc.gov/2025015744
LC ebook record available at https://lccn.loc.gov/2025015745

To Joe Sullivan
my patron of joy

High justice would in no way be debased
if ardent love should cancel immediately
the debts these penitents must satisfy.
                                    —Dante, *Purgatorio*

Contents

PART 1

At the Heart
of a Glowing Universe

I sat in my hotel room in Jackson, Mississippi, waiting to pick up Arthur for his release from prison when the news broke showing the first images of the James Webb telescope. The most stunning of images flashed on my iPhone as I watched the ancient universe premiere live. Images, flush with vibrant colors outlining cosmic dust, gas, and the distant moments of creation, felt like the sudden opening of our history. As I watched, I was struck by a resonance within me between the images of a still-unfolding universe and Arthur's transition from the confines of prison into the outside world.

Arthur, now a young man, had as a child been sentenced to die in prison. After sixteen years of confinement, he was about to be paroled. His extraordinary team of young lawyers—Ashok and Adam, from the Legal Defense Fund, an organization founded by Thurgood Marshall—fought tirelessly to make the unlikeliest thing happen: Arthur's freedom. They knew the odds of Arthur's being granted parole were quite slim in Mississippi.

Yet they managed what could only be described as a modern-day resurrection. After spending over half his life behind bars, Arthur had earned his release—not only through the perseverance of his legal team but through his own determination. He had made the most of the resources and programs available to him in prison, working hard to transform himself from the inside out.

Leaving the hotel, I went to meet Arthur and his lawyers. Together we stood outside the gates of East Mississippi Correctional. Arthur's parents were joyfully at the ready to hold their son again. In a short few minutes Arthur traversed the long walk from the prison, through what is like a loading dock for semitrucks, proceeding to the gates. With each step his smile widened, and he kept pushing back his long curly black hair that kept falling over his face as he picked up his pace.

As soon as he passed through the gates, Arthur was enveloped in the arms of his father, Henry, a tall, lanky man who resembled Frederick Douglass, and his mother, Tina, who embodied the warmth of home. Their embrace lasted a long time—a full, deep hug that seemed to say, "I will never let you go again." It was as if the universe itself had joined in the celebration. The moment felt cosmic—like the explosion of gas and color in the distant reaches of space, a vibrant affirmation of the beauty of life, here on Earth, right now.

Probing this new emergent life, long thought to be confined to the past, a sudden bright light darts onto our Earth landscape. Arthur, just one month after release, was already enrolled in a culinary school and fast on his way to becoming a chef. The kitchen became his canvas. At Joseph House, which I founded as a community for men leaving prison, we all happily promoted his new vocation, devouring delightedly all he brought before us.

Arthur's zest for living free, and each step he now takes as a free man, speaks of a mercy that most of us hope for. Arthur demands we make time for celebrations.

For the past twelve years I have accompanied men whom the state of Florida deemed "the worst of the worst" and of those years, the last six I have lived in community with them—men who have left confinement in Florida's prisons to reenter the world outside. Most have been charged with acts of violence. Some were proven innocent of the charges for which they were imprisoned, while others admitted their guilt. But no matter if they were the so-called worst, violent, innocent, or guilty, they have taught me about goodness in this world, about how porous reality is between us, and about the slow and meandering work of redemption.

This goodness is what philosophers call *being*, physicists call *the universe*, and believers like myself call *God*—the sustaining power behind all that is, all that happens, and all that we do. This goodness often serves as the silently loving backdrop to everything we experience in life. It's the God who wants you to be. Sometimes, this truth comes to me in a sudden moment of clarity, other times quietly and gradually, like a faint whisper in the night. But I have come to trust in a love that endures, originating from God. I've come to know that everything can also fall apart.

My time among the incarcerated, and later at Joseph House with our returning brothers, has slowly taught me that all the explosions and implosions in life call for the sustaining presence of love. I have witnessed the heights of joy restored in men long thought eternally condemned, and I have descended into the depths of rage and violence, bearing witness to a desperation so deep it longs to burn down the whole world. Somewhere in between these extremes, I awoke to a faith, a truth, I can't shake: God prefers mercy, not condemnation. The more we cling to this truth, the more we feel and act in mercy.

Cynicism and fatalism, I've come to believe, are just default defense mechanisms against hope and, perhaps most especially, change. But if we wait a little longer, stay a little quieter, we might notice the smallest of openings for love to find its way into our consciousness.

Somehow, my own gradual awakening to the irrefutable goodness operating in this world coincided with my discovery of that durable goodness within the lives of those labeled by the state as "the worst of the worst." I can't say exactly how it happened, only that it did—and it changed my life.

I learned of a durable love—one that can hold all the complicated emotions we contend with in this life: a love that outlasts shame and guilt, a love that beckons us toward a justice made whole.

This book, my story, is a kind of reflective glass catching and refracting the immanence of light that pervades our shared humanity. Only when we see things differently are we inclined toward working in areas of justice and healing to ensure that every human soul can discover, or rediscover, these fundamental mysteries that lie at the heart of our glowing universe.

The human ingenuity—both the NASA scientist creating such a mind-bending telescope revealing the universe and Arthur's attorneys working long months to reunite Arthur and his parents—made possible this triumph of light through darkness. This communal project between Arthur, his attorneys, and Rachel (our Joseph House social worker) and myself advocating for his admittance into Joseph House seemed to me to be an increasing reliance on the power of love. This universe is awakening along the course of time and in every space unfolding in this universe a God whose love pulsates in a call to greater life.

2

G Wing

In my first two years as a seminarian, I often woke up in the dead of night, gripped by a question that wouldn't let me go: How had I come to be here, in a Roman Catholic seminary, preparing to be a priest. I felt adrift, vocationally lost. I had made significant life decisions to get to this point, but now, doubts crowded in. At thirty-four, I had left a carefully laid path—a doctoral program in religion and philosophy at Florida State University to enter seminary. The life I had known, and the one I was stepping into, both seemed to be unraveling.

In 2013, a few months after defending my dissertation, I would soon begin my pastoral year internship as a seminarian. This is a pivotal year for seminarians, a time to be immersed in the rhythms of parish life, shadowing a priest and discerning whether the priesthood is truly your calling. For many, this year serves as the turning point—when some realize the path to priesthood is not for them. I was already feeling I might be on the verge of making that same decision.

When my pastoral year began, my father was diagnosed with stage-four lung cancer. The cancer, which had started in his lung, had spread to his spine. He became bedridden and heavily sedated, surrounded by my mother, my brothers, and me. I had originally been assigned to a parish in Panama City, but after my father's diagnosis, my bishop reassigned me to a parish in Tallahassee so I could be closer to home.

Having just completed a hospital chaplaincy in Pensacola, I was now living out the very realities I had witnessed from the families I had ministered to in those hospital rooms—watching the certainty of death approach, while keeping vigil by my dying father's side.

When my father's oncologist called to tell me that he had only six to ten weeks left, I fell apart. The call came while I was waiting in the therapist's office, and after hanging up, I walked into my session, the weight of the news still fresh. I sat on the couch and broke down. I had heard people say the best place to fall apart is in a therapy session. It was clear that more than ever I was uncertain about my place in the seminary.

Joan Didion, in her memoir *The Year of Magical Thinking*, writes about the fragility and instability we experience in the aftermath of a significant loss. The world, she observes, becomes unstable, and we feel exposed, uncertain. I had entered my father's illness already feeling that fragility, but now it was magnified.

Grief is a reckoning—a confrontation with death awakening us to the hidden realities of what is ultimate in the universe. It stirs a kind of spiritual tremor, as if we've brushed against the mysterious realm that Rudolf Otto, Lutheran theologian and philosopher, called the *mysterium tremendum*. It is as though, in witnessing the brevity of life, we encounter the numinous: God in all the mystery and glory.

The Catholic funeral mass speaks of life being "changed,

not ended." Perhaps grief, too, is a reorientation of love, a reshaping of how we inhabit the world with this new absence. For me, my father's death was not the end of something, but the transformation of love. His passing triggered a deep, complicated love I hadn't fully realized I had for him. And in that raw, exposed grief, I was brought closer to the truth of that love, even as it broke me open.

Now, with some distance, I see how this experience of fragility opened me to something much larger than myself. The first few weeks into my parish internship I would soon find myself immersed in Florida's prison system.

Slowly, what began to unravel was a hidden truth—a truth I hadn't fully understood before. That God's love flows through all of us, that underneath every human desire is the singular desire to love and to be loved. How we wake up to that reality, how we come to know it in our own stories, well, that's up to each of us. But for me, it began in that painful, fragile space—the space where grief and love intersect, and where, somehow, a more immense calling began to emerge.

The pastor at the parish where I served, Father Michael Foley, an older Irish priest known for his tireless and tender pastoral dedication to his flock at Good Shepherd Church in the suburbs of north Tallahassee, met with me to discuss what my life would look like over the course of the next year. He approached this conversation with a startling question that I was in no way prepared for—"What would you like to do this year?"

I hadn't been asked such an open-ended question from a superior since starting formation back in 2011. Now it triggered a bewildering yet powerful sensation. I can't express how good it felt to be asked this question. There was much resentment and frustration simmering under the surface due to a combination of witnessing my father's declining health and feeling lost and stuck in a vocation I increasingly couldn't see as a fulfilling life. That aching awareness of emptiness one gets when speculating on their place in this world filled me.

I peered into the not-so-distant future to ponder what my life would look like. I was not one enchanted by the fine details of liturgy and canon law. I wasn't thrilled at the prospect of attending endless parish potlucks. I appreciated the pastoral zeal so many priests have for parish life, but it wasn't resonating with me. So, it was incumbent upon me to ask, was I even called to the life of a parish priest? I knew if this was an authentic vocation, it must conjure a transcendent love grounding a life of service. But I was not convinced of my place, my role. As I struggled initially to answer Father Mike's question, a conviction emerged. "Father Mike, I've been confined to the bubble of seminary life, I want to minister also to those outside the parish walls."

He responded in his modest way, gently suggesting I investigate prison ministry if I was interested in deepening my pastoral experience.

"We've got a lot of parishioners who minister in prisons."

But he singled out one parishioner, recommending I connect with Dale Recinella, a lay Catholic chaplain at death row and solitary confinement.

Dale was a sixty-year-old former finance attorney who had spent the previous sixteen years in prison ministry. He ended his career as an attorney so he and his wife Susan could dedicate more time accompanying the marginalized. He was passionate about his work in the prisons in a way that neither idealized nor sentimentalized it—the work was hard and grim. There were plenty of dark nights in his outreach to Florida's most isolated residents. He struck me as one deeply affected by this mission. It had left a mark on him and from that came both his passion and realism.

"I've known folks with full military careers who made one attempt visiting the imprisoned and told me that they couldn't go back. It was too much," he said. Dale looked me in the eye with direct and intense scrutiny—as though to say this may be your outcome as well, and don't take it personally if it is.

He asked questions that made it feel like he was the father of a girl I wanted to date: What were my motivations? What was my agenda? Was I in it for the long haul?

In his considered way, Dale was making sure I understood the extraordinary space I would be entering. My presence would matter to these men—not because I was special, but because they were isolated, confined, and dehumanized, and I would be another human being willing to engage in conversation and relationship with them.

"These are incredibly harsh places, warehousing people with exceptional needs that are barely even acknowledged by staff." Dale paused, and then continued, "It'll affect you, and in ways unwelcome." He wasn't trying to sell me on this ministry. I respected that.

One week later, on a Tuesday evening in early October, together we drove to Florida State Prison (FSP). That night changed me. Looking back, I can trace some of the ways I arrived there, yet nothing could have forecasted the impact it would have on my life.

FSP is in Raiford, just off I-10 on state farmland about twenty-five miles southwest of Jacksonville. To say it is in the middle of nowhere is an understatement. It's a massive, light-green concrete structure standing like a fortress in what they call the Iron Triangle, an ironic reference to the Bermuda Triangle, another place you can get stuck in and never leave. Union Correctional Institution is also in Raiford. The two house all of Florida's death row inmates—about seventy in FSP's G Wing and another three hundred in Union Correctional at that time.

As we neared the prison, Dale briefed me on the details of our visit. With each piece, he hinted at large-scale injustices at play in Florida's justice system. I won't forget that dusk-filled sky hanging over Raiford as we entered the parking area. We both looked out at the horizon to see dark and drifting rain clouds encroaching from the west.

Dale guided me through this maximum-security state prison that October evening, explaining the process in detail as we made our way past various steel-barred electronic gates and security posts. We passed large metal doors that opened into large confinement dorms, housing nearly one hundred men per dorm. The noise was faint yet full of human activity: banging, laughing, yelling.

It took a while to get a sense of my new environment, a far cry from any place I had ever been. But with each step further in, I felt a growing singular sensation that a new task in life was being granted to me.

A strange peace, a portion of confidence and clarity poured into my soul, causing it to expand in multiple directions all at once. Mysteriously, this peace coincided with exposure to people condemned to brutalizing spaces. How does such a paradox even happen? I have no answer, but somehow I found my vocation among those condemned. I had no idea where this would lead me. Only that I must follow, because something awakened inside me that night—a new desire, or perhaps an old desire now transformed.

The huge metal door from G Wing was slammed behind us. The corridor sergeant shut and bolted the door from the outside while the wing officer bolted it from the inside. And there we were, in the quarter deck, with three officers seated at a table. Quarter decks are like the vestibule in the wing.

That night I engaged in multiple conversations, discussing NCAA football, state politics, and the basics of life on the row. These were remarkably ordinary conversations. My initial fear and intimidation faded quickly. It was telling just how familiar all these conversations were. This wasn't like Clarice's fear-stricken walk down the catwalk to meet with Hannibal Lecter. It was far less sensational.

Often these days, I think back on that first walk down the corridor, that incredible moment peace filled my consciousness, as though I had passed through a sustained period of prayer emerging on the other side of those large metal doors filled with ease being with Florida's condemned.

One conversation stood out from that night. My conversation with Tavares.

As I walked to his cell, I could hear he was engaged in, well let's just say, an intense conversation with his neighbor. On G Wing that may mean the fella in the cell next door or a cell fifty yards away. The way prisoners manage to have conversations never ceases to amaze me. Lively discourses often take place through air vents.

Air vents run all through the wing so if one prisoner yells

through the vent in his cell "hey bro in G12," specifying which cell the incoming call is going to, then the prisoner in G12 will jump on his toilet shouting "what's up bro" into the duct. Amidst the constant buzz of noise, somehow detailed conversations can be had between two prisoners through an air vent.

Without missing a beat, Tavares switched conversation partners engaging me immediately.

"What's up preacher man?" Tavares, a hulky Black man in his mid-thirties, speaks in a rapid-fire style that reassures his interlocutor he's fully present and ready to engage.

I get called it all: preacher man, pastor, man of God, exorcist, reverend, prophet; I've even been mistaken for a rabbi by a correctional officer. What followed was a fifteen-minute conversation ranging from religion, theoretical physics, philosophy, to street life in Liberty City.

After I formally introduced myself as a seminarian and explained what that was, Tavares cut to the chase.

"So, you may say *God*, I'll say *the universe;* man there isn't solace here for a soul trying to survive. The state's trying to kill me, I'm on the kill-list, you feel me, pastor. This shit is real."

All I came up with was an unsure, "That sounds pretty accurate to me," but Tavares was not put off. He continued.

"Well, I'm here thinking in my state-designed think tank that the soul saviors of the world are quick to indoctrinate a gangsta like me, but when I ask if they'll spare some time to banter a bit, they disappear as quick as the Holy Ghost."

Tavares ended this with an inquisitive smile, as though to say, give me your best rejoinder, preacher man.

"I'll do my best not to be condescending," I responded.

Tavares spoke that night like a man who didn't have time

for pleasantries. Perhaps he was finished that night with entertaining other folks' religious fantasies. He wanted to know if I could take the direct hits—an intellectually honest conversation.

What then transpired that night between us as I stood in front of Tavares's cell on G Wing changed the trajectory of my life. Like the sudden turning of a ship already deep into ocean currents and moving in one direction to the new coordinates of a different course required something on the level of a calling.

The way Tavares talked about the realities of life on the inside, if you put it into book form, would read like a fast-paced mix between memoir and philosophical commentary with the chronicling of his personal journey through the prison pipeline. That night Tavares opened a window for me to peer into the lives of these men condemned on the row. His words helped me see that the boundlessness of their lives hung suspended in condemnation.

"Listen preacher Dustin," now at least Tavares was using my name, "most of my brothers on the row messed up, they done killed someone or some people, but most of them did so while living a thugged-out or drugged-up life. There's much more to them than the crime they went and did."

"Now don't get it crooked, there are some men here, good God, they scare me and I'm a Liberty City gangsta. But most, nah, they addicts, mentally afflicted, sure, but monsters? No."

As I spent more and more time with men like Tavares, the new world I inhabited became all the more intricate and treacherous yet ready to bestow blessings. These conversations held together their aliveness and their suffering. Hearing Tavares's intensity that night produced a new way of seeing that would have an untold effect on how I would experience the world in the future, as I witnessed goodness in spaces society had effectively demonized.

The world broke free that night from the false equilibrium I insisted on holding and instead heaved and plunged just as the Earth's crust does under our feet. So, too, I experienced this huge rotating world undergoing a change, perhaps a transfiguration of sorts, as I sensed my role opening to assist in its fuller development. I still struggle to make sense of what happened that night, but I can only affirm what Tavares said, *life had become much more real.*

From here on out, among those trapped and forgotten, I would witness such an aliveness bestowed on humanity, and I began to see it continuously, with its untold depths. Here on the G Wing, I felt I had discovered the heart of the world. A heart ablaze in steel, forgotten in confinement.

Maybe this was what the mystic and theologian William of Saint-Thierry referred to as the "midnight silence," the place in the depth of error where we have the power to restore the dignity of others by seeing and hearing them. By witnessing and acknowledging their presence, their presence presents us to God.

That Tuesday evening's visit to FSP would be the first of many. Following that October night, I'd join Dale for weekly visits every Tuesday throughout my pastoral year. Then toward the end of my pastoral year, I managed to convince my bishop to grant me an eight-week immersive internship to join Dale and other volunteers for daily visits.

My time on death row that year confronted me with stories of profound human tragedies and cruelty, yet it also showed me how some individuals, even under the direst circumstances, have managed to transcend the power of condemnation.

I think of Chadwick, who brutally killed his wife and then raped and murdered his stepdaughter. Following an argument with his wife, Cassandra Banks, in a rural town west of Tallahassee, Chadwick returned home inebriated and shot his wife point-blank in the head. His rage continued as he raped, shot, and killed his ten-year-old stepdaughter, Melody Cooper.

There is no way to fully comprehend the grief and pain unleashed by acts of unimaginable violence. How does one begin to forgive such terror? Is redemption or forgiveness even possible after bloodshed? And yet, I have often found myself asking, what if our own humanity is bound up with the humanity of someone like Chadwick?

It was on that first evening in the row that my conversations with these men began—conversations that have continued ever since. Over the past twelve years, I have returned many times to visit them, and some have reached the end of their death sentences. Among them, Chadwick.

Chadwick was a convert to Islam, and his piety was evident in every conversation we had. His religion was a lived one, in word and deed. Despite the horror of his past, there was a quiet dignity about Chadwick—a stillness that spoke of a soul who found peace. He was short in stature, with a deep Southern drawl, and always hospitable during our visits. He had the way of an old soul, marked by small but telling gestures. For instance, during our conversations, he would turn his small fan toward me, despite the sweltering heat in his cell. I would insist that he keep the fan directed at himself, knowing I would soon return to air-conditioned comfort, but Chadwick would not hear of it. He insisted on sharing whatever little comfort he had.

I met Chadwick for the last time two months before his execution. That afternoon, his anxiety was palpable—stirred, no doubt, by the rumor that his death warrant from Governor Rick Scott was imminent. As we spoke, there was an unspoken understanding between us, a sense that this might be our final conversation. And it was.

But it is the part of my time with Chadwick that I continue to carry with me—the part that has never left. Despite knowing that the state would soon come for him, that at any moment guards could lead him to the death house, Chadwick still managed to express his nobility. He thanked me for my visits and offered words of encouragement for my work as a priest. In the shadow of his own death, he was focused not on his fate but on mine. His words were not about him but about me. He showed an incredible capacity for love and grace in a situation where most would expect bitterness or despair.

That afternoon, as we spoke as he awaited news of his pending death warrant, Chadwick looked me in the eye and said, "Dustin, you're going to make a great priest. You're open to talking freely. You're open to people from all walks of life. You listen. Damn, my brother, that goes a long way back here, you hear me?" His words came not from someone who saw himself as only a prisoner but from someone offering spiritual care, hopeful that my vocation would be a fulfilling one.

Chadwick's words remain with me, even though they were spoken over a decade ago. They were words that ordained me. They poured into me, strengthening my discernment of the priesthood. I still look back at that day as the beginning of my ordination. It was in those conversations—with Chadwick, Tavares, and others—that my vocation was drawn out, slowly and powerfully, into the unfolding story I was living in real time.

A few days after our visit, Chadwick received his death warrant, and within the next couple of months, his life was extinguished. But I continue to think of him—the man who, even in the shadow of his own death, was able to show kindness, extend grace, and make room for another's humanity. I cannot help but wonder if, in those final moments Chadwick was living out his redemption. And in some quiet, unspoken way, I believe he found it—not through grand gestures but through simple acts of kindness.

On the day of his execution in November of 2014, I was attending the Wednesday noon Mass at the seminary in Boynton Beach. I arrived an hour early to pray a rosary for Chadwick. At Mass, the first reading that day was from St. Paul's letter to Philemon. This letter, a heartfelt plea for reconciliation, struck me that day in the larger context of Chadwick's pending execution at Florida State Prison. In it, Paul urges Philemon to see Onesimus not as a slave but as a brother. He speaks of a communion, a kinship that now binds them together. The message was profound: forgiveness, reconciliation, and the making of new restored relationships through the power of Christ's Kingdom. The Kingdom of God, Paul reminds us, erases the distinctions that humans often make—whether of class, gender, race, crimes, or status—and calls us into one family, as brothers and sisters in Christ.

As I listened to the reading, I couldn't help but think of Chadwick. No matter what the state deemed him that day, I knew in God's eyes, Chadwick was a brother. While I knew this long before that day, in the context of Mass, the reality felt celebrated in the Kingdom of God. The liturgy that day affirmed this truth: in God's Kingdom, we are all bound together by love.

Chadwick had acknowledged the atrocity he had committed. He was under the influence of drugs at the time, and he took full responsibility for his actions. He didn't deny the gravity of what he had done, and yet he had found peace in God's forgiveness and lived his faith as a devout Muslim. But it didn't matter if he was guilty or innocent, he remained a human being and for that reason alone Chadwick manifested the glory of God.

In that moment, I was reminded of the truly complex and multifaceted nature of priesthood. Through my conversations with men like Chadwick and Tavares—men who had shared their pain, their struggles, and their hopes—I realized that I was not just being called to be a priest. I was being called to be a brother—to offer that love which persists.

3

The Disappeared

"You know, father, our men just kept disappearing."

Levada, the matriarch of Saint Anthony's Catholic Church in Pensacola, spoke to me with a sadness seemingly forged by long rivers of time. She waded into the memories of these disappearances and relayed them to me as we rode in the church bus back from Montgomery to Pensacola.

Levada lived all her eighty plus years of her life in Pensacola. She was an elder in the Black Catholic community, the church sacristan, sang in the choir, and storekeeper of much of the parish's memory. Small and frail, yet with an unmistakable fire in her bones. When she spoke of Jesus, you knew her life was bound to the grace and justice he taught her. When she prayed, you wanted to hold on to the hem of her garment hoping her prayer would cover you too. Her love was fierce, and you knew looking at her that grief and tragedy followed her.

"Our boys, our brothers, our men, Father, one by one they went missing, and we didn't know where they went." With her head shaking you knew the absence of those missing was truly mystifying for her.

These men had disappeared, and their absence created a hole in her life. She added, "The ones that came back, they weren't ever the same."

What Levada communicated to me on that bus ride back to Pensacola was how the great number of men picked up for crimes and sent off to Florida's prisons felt something like what she and I witnessed earlier that day at a parish-organized trip to Montgomery, Alabama, to visiting the National Museum for Peace and Justice and the Lynching Memorial. What we saw in the exhibits, newsreels, and photos was the legacy of racial terror—and what Levada had witnessed for most of her life, while it may not have been the barbaric lynchings we saw memorialized, it was the precipitous disappearance of Black men from local communities equaling the precipitous increase of Black men incarcerated in the state of Florida prisons.

Three years later, now a Catholic priest in Florida's Panhandle, I routinely was entering prisons, witnessing how the further disappearance of countless Black men was happening systemically through solitary confinement.

Santa Rosa Correctional, on the western end of Florida's Panhandle, is a massive solitary confinement camp. Ministers are permitted to go where other outsiders are not in a high-maximum-security prison. Visitors see the visitation room near the entrance to the facility, just past the well-manicured front lawns and gleaming razor wire fences. They are kept away from the sweltering dorms (many of Florida's prisons are without AC) where over one thousand men are warehoused in solitary confinement. In the steel and concrete hallways lined with steel cells, men swelter in the summer heat, idle and bored. It is a landscape without aliveness into which men with nothing to hope for are systematically packed. They've got it down to a science in our state correctional system. A bad science, and often terribly mismanaged, but a science, nonetheless.

I moved slowly along these hallways, sweating and uncomfortable in the stench and constant jarring noise, year after year, from cell to cell, noting countless blank stares of hopelessness and defeat. It has been my practice to stop at each of the scratched plexiglass windows to inquire about each man's life, his hopes, and desires for his future. It felt sometimes as if I'd been entrusted with the scroll of life asked to be read anew. One of those locked away in solitary confinement was Malachi.

Malachi's story isn't unique among the prison population, especially those in confinement. Malachi has a life sentence for a murder charge. A thirtyish Black man from central Florida, his face awash in tattoos; when he smiles, it's as though a graffiti wall suddenly morphs into a human face.

Growing up in largely violent and impoverished communities has many like Malachi with little to no sense of agency and no meaningful way to access the mainstream. Life in a gang was inevitable, the only social world available, as inevitable as jumping from shelter to shelter, or sleeping from couch to couch. Malachi's world before his life sentence was filled with a bewildering chaos.

"Father, I robbed, I stole from people, I stayed in detention facilities probably more than I went to school."

Malachi spoke with such clarity that I think he must've reflected on this at length. He spoke of his father's abandonment and then how his older brother committed a double murder suicide.

As Malachi spoke about the petty crimes he had committed, there was something else beneath his words—an underlying misery that seemed to shadow him.

"I've carried a lot of pain, anger, and aggression since I was a kid, growing up in a single-parent household."

It struck me how Malachi described his childhood: almost like a statistic, as if his struggles were part of some larger, impersonal narrative. The way he spoke—matter of fact, distant—made it clear that this was a story he'd lived over and over, a story that had long since lost its shock value for him.

Malachi would recount his murder to me as though we were in the confessional—both of us kneeling on the grimy concrete floor, separated by a steel door in the D Dorm at Santa Rosa Correctional. I thought it was telling that Malachi spoke of his murder not as an isolated moment but just one step in an ongoing sequence of other moments: a thread in a seamless garment. My ear up to the flap, where food trays are usually delivered, Malachi shared with me a detailed and intimate accounting of both his life and his crime.

My knee was nearly numb from kneeling on the concrete at this point, but Malachi was not done. He was saying vulnerability led him to the streets. But what he meant by *vulnerability* was different than most of us. Vulnerability is a simple fact of existence, especially during childhood. It can be something good when dependency involves trusted others who show us love. But a vulnerability awakened by aggression at the hands of someone stronger cripples all semblance of normal development—it begets rage and distorts everything about our view of the world. The truism that hurt people hurt people becomes truth.

As I could no longer bear kneeling, Malachi came to the

crime that had landed him a life sentence. It was one night when Malachi, in the thralls of a massive psychotic break, became convinced his friend's son was a demon. He told a story like so many I hear. Violent memories and primal emotions play off each other: jolted by drugs and alcohol, one triggering the other until a rush of delusional thoughts and the conviction of invincibility propels him to enact a psychotic fantasy . . . to slay a child.

The night before Malachi murdered a child, his mother and friends tried to have him admitted to a hospital. He was denied admission because he didn't have insurance. The following day Malachi, convinced he was God, stabbed his friend's son in the chest.

I looked at Malachi, and I saw a person trapped. His life now forever defined in this world by that night he, in a psychotic, delusional rage, took the life of child. To be a child killer is the unspeakable crime. Malachi confessed this horrific crime to me as we knelt at the door to his cell, and in that moment, I was lost. My contact with this evil act was barely a brush, and yet it paralyzed me. I didn't know what to say, I could only affirm I heard him. I remember thinking, *You're doomed in this life, poor Malachi. How can such a life ever be restored?* Babylon has this effect. And yet I had to snap out of the hopelessness he had, as it were, poured into me. I could hear his deep regret and how he resented his mental afflictions.

"I hate myself, Father," Malachi said quietly.

He wasn't well. I knew this. How do we restore Malachi? I freely admit I don't know. But we must dream of a time when those who have fallen the lowest may experience restoration, where they may be forgiven and loved for who they are, not held in contempt for what they did.

///

I can't think of any better commentator on life in these confinement dorms than Pre. Pre served a twenty-two-year sentence, ten of which were in solitary confinement.

Pre had also been in solitary confinement at Santa Rosa. And now he lived at Joseph House. Early one cold January morning as I was driving him to his new job, I asked what's the perception of prison by most prisoners in confinement, figuring he would know better than most, since he spent ten years in solitary confinement.

"Are you serious? Most of us see it as a hellhole. Because it is." Pre looked over at me, shocked I'd ask that question.

Pre's a forty-year-old Black man with an exceedingly like-able personality that can narrate a trip to the library and spin it into an epic adventure story filled with multiple wonders. Whenever I finished a lengthy conversation with him, I felt like I had to sweep up all the adjectives and adverbs that spilled out into my room after we spoke. Without a doubt Pre could've made a career in television commentary—whether it be news or sports; this man can impose narrative and plot and full-fledged characters to any life circumstance.

"You got to understand two different groups determine prison life, the justice system with their lock 'em up and throw away the key. 'They animals' type of bullshit. And then you got the lifers and those with Buck Rogers sentences."

I think to myself, *he didn't just refer to that 1970s sci-fi character.*

"Buck Rogers?" I asked. "As in space man? What do you mean Buck Rogers, did I hear you right?"

"Yeah, those are the ones who might not have life sentences

but might as well. They are getting out in 2040, 2050, 2145, 2380."

"Now I got it. Their freedom is in sci-fi realm, so far in the future it might as well be fantasy."

"Right. So, with all that, you got a system totally broken no one believes in it, especially the officers, and then you got these people who know, they know, they'll never see freedom in this life so they're just like fuck it. They think nothing matters, and consequences don't matter either."

Pre continued, "You got to understand, and I know you've experienced some of this yourself, these dorms are where men get served air trays for lunch, meaning there isn't a damn thing on the tray. Hell, I've seen men get served a dead rat before. Or another torture technique might be spraying Black Jesus on folks."

Ok, first Buck Rogers, now Black Jesus. I simply asked, "What's Black Jesus"?

"It's a thirty-two-ounce black can of some chemical shit they'd spray on people," Pre said with his head shaking in disgust.

This is it: prison life in Florida is a zero-sum game.

Any world that is utterly corrupt and unruly has opposing it a God who stands outside of it—blemished by its troubled and impossible realities—annihilating the corruption and repairing the chaos. The unruliest, those deemed the most violent, "the worst of the worst," permanently hang suspended in a state of judgment in a world that is frozen in time. With no movement toward a livable future. They are now alien children inhabiting a strange nonworld. These are so many of the faces I see behind these Plexiglas windows, many with Buck Rogers sentences. These are the ones that usually sink to the bottom of Florida's prisons, least likely to have any meaningful engagement with educational or vocational programs.

What I have routinely found in these prison camps is a kind of living death. Yet, and this is where I encounter a trace of something transcendent, there are faint echoes of hope heard in the dreams and aspirations among those condemned in these societal morgues, as it were. In this harsh landscape, gradually I found myself accepting their frailty as my own.

Nearly everything Malachi and the hundreds of thousands of others experience while incarcerated is further shame and cruelty: the debased living conditions, the constant swelling of people warehoused within them, the nauseating food many wouldn't even inflict on their pets, the prison violence as some of society's most traumatized are packed in with each other in one long survivalist situation, the jeering and prodding by many but not all the guards, the condescending and moralizing so many ministers heap on the exiled—all of this reminds me of God's fury against the Babylonians for their treatment of exiled Israel.

At this point, I feel it's important to say a word about prisons in general. I know there will be those who argue that by discussing this, I'm somehow turning those who have committed serious crimes into victims. They might accuse me of disregarding the violence that takes place within prison walls—violence directed at other prisoners and guards by those who are violent themselves. I understand those concerns, and I want to acknowledge them fully. There are indeed many valid concerns for safety and protection because of the violence many have created. They've caused real and lasting harm to others and to their communities. I acknowledge this.

And yet, when I reflect on the prisons I've visited for more than a decade, I see them not as places of justice, or even deterrence for that matter, but as a resounding failure—failure to protect the incarcerated, failure to protect the prison staff, and ultimately, failure to protect all of us. In thinking about men like Malachi and the conditions under which they live, I am compelled to believe that these institutions cry out for a fundamental reimagining—spaces not for punishment, but for repair. Spaces that take the possibility of mercy seriously.

But the reality in Florida's prisons is far from anything that could be described as repairable. The conditions are so dehumanizing, so entrenched in violence, that it feels nearly impossible to imagine them becoming locales of healing. This is where Father Gregory Boyle's words ring true: "Prisons have become places of organized abandonment." This phrase cuts to the heart of the issue. These institutions aren't just failing to rehabilitate, they are actively abandoning people. They've become places where both the incarcerated and those who work there are left to fend for themselves in a system that seems to care for no one.

4

Master Dreamers

When I began visiting prisons, I noted many of the men would reference the Hebrew Bible's story of Joseph, the son of Jacob, and refer to Joseph as a brother.

Joseph was young when he was thrown in a pit and forgotten. I often think of Joseph as the first to become *the disappeared.*

He was taken into captivity in a foreign land far from his father and mother and made to feel very low and utterly forgotten. One of the more disturbing aspects of Joseph's story is how his brothers not only conspired to kill him in an act of fratricide but how they then proceeded to cast him away without any noticeable sign of remorse. It was as though he no longer existed. Decades would pass before they would acknowledge their own guilt in selling their brother into slavery.

Joseph was a dreamer, like so many of the men I visited. Though often sunk by despair, wading deep in the waters of loneliness, these men I would visit in those early months would talk about how they found themselves dreaming of a life where they are reconciled with their families, their communities, their friends, and some even with their victims.

One example was Andrá, whom I visited at Wakulla Correctional fifteen miles south of Tallahassee. During our visits in the chapel, he spoke of Joseph tenderly, as someone who shared his own experience.

Andrá once told me, "You know how with Joseph, every setback, every seeming failure, it seems like he's even more gone than gone itself; yet like an all-star, he keeps coming back with even bigger dreams!"

As I was listening to men like Andrá, I, too, found myself starting to dream dreams I had not dreamt before—for community, for belonging. Talking with close friends and parishioners engaged in prison ministry, we started thinking about how to create a space where many of these men could be restored back to us.

As we talked, all of us kept going back to the story of Joseph, realizing how pivotal Joseph hosting his brothers for dinner in his house played. It was at the table memories, thought forgotten, found their way to the surface, and reconciliation was able to take place. Joseph's brothers had to embrace the bitter truth of harming and neglecting their brother, but this led to mercy and forgiveness unheard of in ancient literature, with love washing over the years of hurt and loneliness.

The story of Joseph conjured for us an ideal to work toward. It became a story we imagined could be retold in our own land and in our own time.

///

Qwan, a twenty-two-year-old Black man, looked more like fifteen with his scrawny stature and dimpled face. He was incarcerated for an assault with a deadly weapon. Qwan, like many, to escape further violence and abuse had intentionally caused disciplinary incidents, which placed him in solitary confinement.

I had visited him a couple of times, and one day he informed me he was going to be released soon. When that day came, he would be led out of his cell, transported to the local bus station, and given a ticket to travel to his designated drop-off.

I asked, "Where's home, where do you plan to return to?"

Qwan's answer came off unsure.

"Home's in Tallahassee, so Tallahassee I guess."

"Do you have a game plan for when you leave here?"

"No, not really."

And then he shrugged, and the edge of a smile lifted his mouth as if to say, "Do you have a game plan for me?"

As we continued to talk that day; it was evident Qwan had no idea how or where he would live once he left prison. All he could see at that time was leaving. He had, at best, a fifty-fifty chance of staying out of prison for the first year of his release, and the odds were two to one he would be back in prison in three years. Statistically speaking, his chances of staying out of prison were grim. I decided to get involved in his reintegration after release.

Qwan's release date was set for Sunday May 20, 2018—which happened to be Emancipation Day in the state of Florida. This was wonderful news; however, there was one problem. Due to my Sunday Mass obligations in the outreaches of the Panhandle, I would not be available to meet him at the bus station. After making my commitment to assist Qwan in his journey back home, I needed to find someone else to do that.

My awareness of these needs led me to call Sonya. I mentioned to her the dilemma of not having anyone to pick up Qwan upon his return. Sonya and her husband, Brian, had been friends of mine since the mid-1990s. We had already journeyed through life together through tragedies and celebrations. I knew their values and they mine. In our daily ritual of catching up over the phone, I voiced my concern that no one would be there for Qwan when he arrived at the bus station. She didn't bite, at least not verbally. Later she acknowledged that she knew her husband Brian would have serious reservations. And understandably so.

In this work I have come to respect people's limitations when accompanying those charged with criminal offenses. And by limitations, I mean the limits to know what they in good faith can and cannot do. I think more damage will be done if people agree to meet a need without, at the same time, feeling convinced it is the safe or even the right thing to do. In this case in fact, after Sonya recounted our conversation to Brian, he had reservations. The idea, after all, was to pick up a stranger at the bus station who had just completed three years in prison for an assault with a deadly weapon. Who wouldn't be on edge with this invitation? If Brian wasn't apprehensive, there'd be reason for concern about his judgment! But because of our friendship and because Sonya had come to feel it was the right thing to be there for Qwan, Brian agreed to pick up Qwan with her.

Sonya and Brian were preparing to meet Qwan at the Tallahassee bus station. When I showed Sonya a picture of him, she was surprised how young he was. She noted that he did not look like a hardened criminal.

Qwan had been told I would not be meeting him, but rather friends of mine. After departing the bus, he should go into the station where they would be waiting. When the bus pulled in, stopped, and opened its doors, he and the other passengers moved down the steps.

Sonya identified him from the station but was surprised when he only briefly glanced in that direction and then proceeded to move down the side of the building rather than entering. Leaving Brian in the station, Sonya ran out to find Qwan. She got about five feet from him.

She called softly, "Hey, are you Qwan?"

He turned, paused momentarily, and then smiled broadly. His smile reflected his joy at being recognized, being seen by another.

"Yes ma'am, I'm Qwan."

Speaking later, Qwan explained he had figured no one would be there for him when he got off the bus. He did not want to compound the feeling of being abandoned and on his own by entering the bus station, looking around, and coming up empty. He, like me, had likely believed real change wasn't possible.

Over the next few months, as good as it felt to assist Qwan with his reentry into society, it became apparent, if we fully wanted to accompany the released prisoner, we would need a dedicated home to do so.

Discussions had begun, and a few dear friends generously donated a couple of thousand dollars as seed money for what we had decided to call Joseph House. However, I was at a loss on how to proceed, from raising money to deciding on a location and understanding the laws and regulations on opening such a home.

Many years ago, before priesthood, I remembered reading

a story in the local newspaper about Chuck White, along with a resident philanthropist, spearheading an initiative to bring a holistic, wrap-around service to Tallahassee to help the homeless. Their work culminated in the establishment of the Renaissance Center.

One day, I was in a meeting with leaders in city planning and development when Chuck's name was mentioned as someone to consult with for my Joseph House initiative. He was working with the city on ways to provide dignified housing and employment for the formerly incarcerated and homeless. We set up a meeting at a local coffee shop. It turned out I did not need to try to win him over on the idea of Joseph House. He was already all in because he had firsthand experience of the many obstacles faced by those returning from prison.

The best way to describe Chuck is a dreamer—one who has the tenacity, skills, and enthusiasm to make dreams come true. He first elevates your expectations, then helps you bring them to reality. I explained to him where things currently stood. City managers were coaxing us to consider locations in low-income, high-crime areas where most of Tallahassee's formerly incarcerated lived. They were clear this would be a long process, involving knocking on doors and obtaining the support of community leaders. They estimated it would be two to three years before we would be able to purchase a house.

Chuck said forget all of that. "Father, the last place you want your home for these men coming out of prison is down the street from the corners where many of them were picked up and arrested."

Chuck continued, emphatically, "You want a place near good jobs, a place in an area that will not remind them of the criminal circuits they are familiar with, a place they can walk to work if needed and not feel monitored by either drug dealers or law enforcement."

What Chuck was saying is you want them to feel as though they are ordinary citizens, going about their daily life free from unsafe entanglements.

Chuck raised the bar and said, "Father let's look for a house in a nice area, in close proximity to the city's commerce, that can effectively offer these men a new start."

He explained it would not be easy navigating the multiple city ordinances and zoning restrictions on top of the push-back we would receive. However, it could be done, and much sooner than the city's estimate given me.

Therefore, we began a search for a home in earnest. Demonstrating his skills as a semiretired developer and utilizing his connections, I received a call from Chuck two months into the search.

"Father, I think we may have found our house."

It was a one-story home built in 1957 on the slope of one of Tallahassee's hills. It was in a good location and could accommodate three people, with the potential to remodel a carport into additional rooms in the future. The next step would be to meet with the head of the Diocese of Pensacola–Tallahassee, Bishop Bill Wack, to confirm he was on board to move forward to make the purchase, moving Joseph House from a concept to a reality.

The meeting took place in January 2019 in a conference room at Saint Thomas More Cathedral. Chuck was frank with the bishop.

"Now I want you to know upfront, Bishop, that we may get serious pushback from the city if we buy this house," Chuck warned. He said, "The last thing the Church or you need is bad front-page headlines condemning the Catholic Church for housing violent offenders in our safe communities."

Chuck went on to clarify. "Bishop, it's important you know that midtown Tallahassee is a very desirable location and developing quickly both commercially and residentially. Your bringing a halfway house into this area is a threat to their capital. They want us in areas already overrun with social services and far from the high-tax bracket areas. So, this is your decision. You just need to know the hard facts before signing onto this."

I winced: Chuck's narrative even put doubts in my own mind. I knew Bishop Wack had a big, generous heart for the poor and marginalized, but I was concerned this might be a bridge too far for him to cross.

It was a moment of silence that seemed to last many minutes. Bishop looked at me and then at Chuck, and said with confidence, "But this is the gospel, to welcome the stranger, so we must think according to the gospel. Let's get this house."

I do not think even the word *ecstasy* adequately describes my feeling in that moment. I thought, here is the Church in action—making decisions with the needs of the poor, the imprisoned, the outcast first in in mind. It was as though for a moment justice was possible in ways not even I had expected.

It was sweltering in the Florida heat as Qwan and I drove through Tallahassee, hopping from one errand to the next. The humidity of the summer days here was like a blanket that seemed to smother the city. We were both thirsty, and I figured a couple of icy drinks from the gas station would help us cool off. Pulling into the lot, I left the car running, thinking only for a moment about whether I should turn the engine off or leave it on.

In those few seconds, an unexpected thought flickered: *Should I turn off the car and let Qwan sit in the heat while I ran inside, or should I leave the AC running, keeping him cool while I went in for the drinks?* The thought was strange, almost unwelcome, and for a second, I felt guilty for even thinking it. After a moment of indecision, I chose the simpler path—I left the key in the ignition and the air conditioning blasting.

When I came back to the car, drinks in hand, I shifted into reverse, ready to continue our day. As we started to pull out of the parking spot, Qwan looked over at me and said, "Damn man, you don't know how much it meant to me that you left the car running while you went inside the store. That felt good, dude." And Qwan wasn't talking about the AC.

In an instant I understood what prompted Qwan to say this. Just a few weeks earlier, I had begun accompanying Qwan after his release from solitary confinement at Santa Rosa Correctional. He had been charged with a violent offense, and I think he'd come to expect that people would be suspicious of him, that they would assume the worst. He had internalized a version of himself that made him feel untrustworthy in the eyes of others.

To be trusted in this small, seemingly insignificant way—entrusted with the keys to my car—felt like something much larger. It was a gesture of care, a subtle but powerful acknowledgment that he was capable of being trusted. I realized then that for Qwan, this small act was a sign that he was being seen differently, that there was the possibility of a new way of relating to the world, a way where he wasn't defined by the assumptions of others.

I suspect that when we know we are trusted, we also begin to feel we are loved.

※

Journey is movement. It incorporates moments of doubt and darkness. For progressing along the way will entail moments of uncertainty. A journey is traveling from one place to another while also suggesting a difficult process of personal change.

One reason journey works when thinking about serving those leaving prison is because it forgoes any solutionism that predetermines our task as mainly there to fix people. Sadly, many social services agencies and faith-based ministries seem fixated on outcomes, success stories, and solutions. A truly human journey does not stress predetermined outcomes—rather it emphasizes an unfixed period that it takes to get from one place to another place. It also gives the connotation of a story unfolding in that process. Not a story for a specific idea to be vouched for or a goal to be accomplished; rather a story to be lived. More importantly, a story eventually to be told.

We are all compiling a travelogue through the varieties of life stages and the experiences that shape us. We all have an origins story. Most of us have instances of feeling exiled and alone. We all have destinies we imagine ourselves arriving to in life that usually include the people we love and places we call home.

One day Andrá said to me as we sat in the chapel at Wakulla Correctional. "Father Dustin, the things we can do together to bring some people who need light here, well that means you're going to need to dream even bigger."

With Andrá, with the Joseph House work, I've become

convinced that dreams open new vistas for us to imagine ourselves and the world we inhabit. Alone, these dreams may falter to mere fantasy; but shared with a community these dreams of ours—and their attendant joys—may change the world.

5

Superpowers

Shortly after my ordination to the priesthood in 2016, while assigned to serve at the cathedral in Pensacola, I met one of the deacons there, John Parnham. A retired circuit judge of Escambia County, John was a compassionate man and wore a warm smile more than occasionally.

As I came to know John that year, he opened up about what he perceived to be serious injustices in the criminal justice system, particularly racial injustices. One day he and I took a trip up to the Equal Justice Initiative's law offices in Montgomery. There we met with Maria Morrison, the senior social worker at EJI and a few other staff attorneys. EJI, a private, nonprofit organization is rooted in the principles of the civil rights movement and human rights. They provide legal advocacy and social services for the poor, the incarcerated, the condemned, and children sentenced to lengthy sentences. EJI has brought much assistance to juveniles condemned to die in prison.

As we met with Maria and another staff attorney, they relayed how many policymakers in the 1970s believed the prison population in the United States was too large at

200,000. Fifty years later the number is alarming, with 2.3 million people incarcerated. Maria cited statistics of "the Bureau of Justice finding that one in three Black male babies born today will spend time in prison at some point in their lifetimes. In 2016, Black males ages eighteen and nineteen were twelve times as likely as White males of the same age to be imprisoned."

What John and I heard on that Thursday afternoon was horrifying. Within those numbers are further horrors, including the extreme brutality that many incarcerated undergo in our state's custody. Yet with groups like EJI, there's hope. There are witnesses to the injustices, and it's not going unnoticed. Maria and others spoke on the challenges for those reentering society, especially some of their clients. Listening to them, I felt like I'd finally found people who could understand and advocate for those who faced vast human rights abuses in these prison slums in Florida.

John opened up at one point, telling Maria how sorry he was to have participated in such a horrifically biased justice system. I had come to know John toward the end of his career and knew he worked tirelessly to create diversion programs, shifting cases from incarceration to drug courts and rehabilitative services. But it was clear he felt his hands were stained from participating in Florida's justice system.

As John and I left the EJI building, he said to me, "Father, slavery is alive and well."

///

A few months after our visit to EJI, Maria mentioned an EJI client, Joe Sullivan, saying he might be someone to consider as Joseph House's first resident now that we had a home we'd soon move into. On a late July day in 2018, we met Joe for pizza near the EJI offices. From the start, Joe was ebullient. "How ya doing, my friend?" Joe—JoJo—gave a thumbs up sign, his statement meaning I come in peace.

It seemed as though I'd known Joe for years; old friends seeing each other after a long hiatus. But that was the first time we met, on that summer day. Yet, I sensed an immediate connection as though something good were unfolding. That's how providence works; it's that heavy dose of goodness right from the start combined with another full dose of energy needed for accomplishing the task ahead of us.

I learned that Joe is my age, and due to advanced MS, he uses a wheelchair. But any encounter with Joe reveals his superior imagination and shows you how easy it is for him to dream as he invites you into a vision for the future. Being with Joe, it becomes easier for you to dream as well. His enthusiasm and his vision made him the ideal companion for this journey ahead of us in building a community for those orphaned by the justice system.

Joe spoke of his familiarity with the fear and vulnerability I've witnessed in so many of the imprisoned. "I was thirteen when they took me away from my family," Joe recounted.

In this case, "they" was the state of Florida. Bryan Stevenson, his attorney and the founder of EJI, shared his story in the powerful book, *Just Mercy.* In 1989, a woman was brutally raped in Pensacola by a man she was unable to facially recognize. But two older boys implicated the young boy Joe as the perpetrator. These two boys and Joe had been at this woman's house earlier in the day intending to rob it. Joe confessed he was present for the robbery but repeatedly denied committing sexual battery. Joe to this day remains steadfast in his innocence of the sexual battery charges that resulted in him receiving a life sentence without parole. Many others, including myself, believe this young man was in fact innocent.

Joe is one of only two thirteen-year-olds in the country given such judgment.

I thought of the differences in our stories. In late 1988, I, too, was thirteen, a young kid in a middle-class home, debating whether to get my ear pierced and hoping to get a part in the upcoming production of *A Christmas Carol* at my middle school in Birmingham's southside suburbs. Just a few months apart, Joe, also thirteen, was condemned to die in prison by an adult jury—this after his having lived a semihomeless life throughout early adolescence. By his thirteenth birthday Joe was already caught up in the system. If all this coming at him at his young age weren't outrage enough, consider that Joe's early years were filled with abuse and neglect. But Joe's judge paid no attention to the suffering and neglect of Joe's young life—as though those things just didn't matter.

At the trial in the Escambia County courthouse, the judge showed his disregard for Joe's early life of semihomelessness and abuse. The judge said, "I'm going to send him away for as long as I can."

When a man robed in justice, ordained by the state, and esteemed by his community, calls upon the gods of law and order to say such a thing of a thirteen-year-old, it's madness. How did this man feel to speak JoJo's existence away like that? Joe was offered up as sacrifice for the sake of public safety to the gods of law and order. *Cruelty* is the name this evil form of sorcery takes.

And the judge was part of a larger system. Florida hid a long history of state-supported abuse toward children, including the infamous Dozier School for Boys currently lying abandoned in Marianna, where it looks to all the world like a concentration camp.

Florida is notorious for trying and sentencing children as adults. In fact, during 2017 and 2018 alone, 904 children were processed through Florida's adult criminal justice system. Add to this already ghastly statistic that three out of four of those children tried as adults were either African American or Hispanic.

When young Joe entered Florida's adult prison system at Lake Butler Correctional at age thirteen, one of his first encounters was with a prison guard with a mean face and chew-spit in in his mouth who said to the young boy, "From now on, I'm your mama and your daddy." Not a statement of care or concern, the guard's words were frightening as if to say, "You have no mother or father here. You are an orphan, and you are now alone." This child. Joe, sent by the state of Florida to die in prison.

Maria and I often discussed reentry, the criminal justice system, and the challenges that those released face as Joe was preparing to come to Joseph House. Her own generous person-centered approach in working with those who have endured a brutal justice system was a gift to witness. And her framing of the cruel realities those surviving the Department of Corrections in Florida had to suffer informed my future work in this area.

While I began with hunches and intuitions, a potent yet undefined sense of the evil that those in prison faced, the structured and concretely stated insights Maria shared with me, as well of her grasp of not only the legal and social hurdles facing the imprisoned, and those to be released, made her a superior interlocutor.

I recalled one conversation with her, in which she said, "Allow the care and concern of others to catch you and engage you, to look into the oblivion with you, as you look into it with the men you visit." Her poetic invitation and encouragement helped me stay attentive to the indignation I felt at seeing so many human injustices in the justice system. But even more than that I received her words as an invitation to watch as the outrage shifted from fury toward a more thoughtful care for those nearly buried underneath all the shame and abandonment.

By May of 2019, the Joseph House staff and JoJo were moved into Joseph House in Midtown Tallahassee. Joe understood the move as his being sent on a mission by Bryan Stevenson to help establish Joseph House. I trust the company of heaven celebrated this mission and his willingness to participate as we did.

One morning during our sharing around our breakfast table at Joseph House, Joe retold the events of his sentencing to our MSW intern Rachel and myself. "That judge thought he had the last word," Joe said. "But oh noooo [Joe waved his finger triumphantly in the air with a smile of victory]; God had the last word and now I'm free!"

The first two to move in were Joe and our social work intern, Tyler. That first week in the summer of 2019 the two became housemates. And their friendship consecrated the space.

We began our trips to Tallahassee's Senior Center with Joe in the summer of his arrival. In those early days Tyler would accompany Joe to all sorts of fun events in Tallahassee. In the months that followed they'd go to softball, baseball, and basketball games. Other volunteers like Sonya and Cecille would celebrate life together with Joe, going to the circus, bowling, big birthday parties, a Boyz II Men concert, and a Filipino breakfast at one of the parishes. What began in those early days at Joseph House was a journey together. And we made it a point to enjoy good things together.

Joe was right there in his appreciation. He has this magical capacity to play. Never mind all the terror, all the abuse cruel folks have thrown JoJo's way; this man contains a secret power this world can't take away. Over the years I've worried about overloading those I'm accompanying with hope. I don't want to increase their troubles with unrealistic dreams that may only further exacerbate their reluctance to trust and believe the world will open its hidden treasures to them. My caution is probably warranted and may even be healthy. But Joe has also taught me that when it comes to hope, sometimes caution needs to be thrown out the window.

For instance, on Friday morning my prayer time was periodically broken up by uproarious fits of joy with Joe rediscovering Knight Rider in the living room. In his wheelchair in front of our TV at Joseph House, Joe watched as Kitt, the talking car in the '80s show, blasted the bad guys away. Joe clapped his hands in victory as nearby I was seated on my futon, praying the breviary, reading, "Thus did God disarm the principalities and power."

///

My time among the incarcerated has led me to sustained meditations on exile, captivity, return, redemption, and reparations as depicted in Israel's psalms and prophets. Those codas of despair and disorientation, of hope and unrestrained desire for freedom, echo the spiritual state of the incarcerated. My work wouldn't have developed as it has without these spiritual hymns and prophetic oracles that unlock otherwise hidden dimensions of our world. These ancient Hebrew scriptures narrate an understanding of this world, and its depths speak of a justice it is created for.

It's no surprise that the French historian and philosopher René Girard surmised these are perhaps the earliest texts in human history where the victim and the vanquished take center stage in the drama of redemption. The history of the psalms is not told from the vantage point of the victors, but instead the Hebraic poems chronicle the interior lives of the oppressed. These stories imbue the sacredness each of us carries within, revealing how the more personal, the more intimate aspects of our lives are often stories waiting to be told. The difficult things we deal with as human beings—those troubling symptoms so many of us contend with—are stories we feel are untellable. But in these texts, they are told.

Within the text it is the orphan who stands out with stories most applicable to those I have encountered in Florida's prisons. Throughout sacred scripture, but most especially in the Hebrew Bible, we hear of the fatherless, the orphan as being the one whom God pays the most attention to, as well as widows. It is the plight of the orphan that seems to make the demand for justice all the more urgent, as though God's righteousness depended on it. Throughout the psalms we hear of the orphan and we hear that God is their helper.

In today's world of mass incarceration, this ancient category finds a type of moral, or perhaps even political, relevance once again. Orphanhood catches all the complexities that befall so many of the men I have witnessed locked up behind cold steel bars and razor-sharp fences. Nearly all of the men whose stories are told in these pages come short of a self-sufficient or independent life. The poverty that swallowed them and the violence that threatened them at a young age denied them opportunities to access social goods afforded to most of us.

Living in community these past six years with Joe and others has brought me close to the edge of the majestic geysers of unrestricted joy as Joe's explosions of joy unleash primordial powers that annihilate destructive forces. In itself, this joy is a natural wonder right here on Bradford Road in Tallahassee.

Joe is hands down the heart of our community. He's eminently sociable, and he exudes a warmth that is almost physical. His body often quakes mightily at the discovery of yet another moment of absurdity. His joy for life is a thing of beauty to behold and is testament against the cruelty of the state of Florida. This man, who has intellectual disabilities and lives wheelchair-bound with MS, has a talent for the type of magic that dispels gloom and incants joy.

When I see Joe's joyous convulsions as the bad guys are vanquished, I'm attuned to where these hard-won joys emerge from, and all the rejection of his earlier life. I recall how Joe's freedom was won by Bryan Stevenson and his team of lawyers at the Equal Justice Initiative. They took Joe's case all the way to the US Supreme Court, which ultimately overturned his life sentence, deeming it cruel and unusual punishment.

But Joe began the urgent work of repairing in so many ways. In the early weeks at Joseph House, Joe even forged a strong alliance with the neighborhood squirrels. Joe would look for food to feed them and would set it out on our back deck. This became a daily ritual at Joseph House.

When I asked Joe about it, he broke it down for me.

"They are God's creatures. It's a circle, you see. God takes care of us and we take care of the squirrels. It's a circle," Joe affirmed, drawing a circle in the air.

In that moment it all became a bit clearer to me. Our community should be defined by the needs of others and how best we can care for their needs.

Joe's capacity to reimagine a world far more loving than the one given to him as a child—well, I think of it as Joe's superpower.

One such superpower moment unfolded when I drove Joe to the Senior Center in midtown Tallahassee. Time felt tight, the minutes slipping away faster than I could manage, and I found myself growing increasingly irritable. On top of that, a heavy sense of hopelessness lingered over me as I watched the Joseph House bank account steadily drain, with the demands and costs involved. During it all, Joe, as always, was his usual self—calm and unaffected.

As my concerns grew and as we drove, Joe then reached for the radio and put on Louis Armstrong's *What a Wonderful World*. At first, I was distracted, caught up in my worries, but then I heard Joe begin to sing along with Louis, his voice light and cheerful. Reluctant at first, I soon found myself singing, too:

> I see trees of green, red roses too,
> I see them bloom for me and you,
> and I think to myself, what a wonderful world.

By the time the song reached its joyful conclusion, Joe glanced at me and, with his characteristic warmth, said, "You know something, Papa, the world is wonderful!"

My heart settled into Jojo's Zen time zone. I smiled and replied, "You're right, Joe, this world is wonderful."

In that fleeting moment, I could only affirm Joe's sentiment with awe. He had a way of embodying the light of the world, even amid his own suffering. It shone through the limitations of his body and through his wide, infectious smile—like a beacon refracting the unseen light of creation itself.

Joe's capacity for joy, for laughter, and for celebration has become a striking counterpoint to the cynicism and brutality of our criminal justice system. On one trip to visit family in Mississippi, we passed the exit sign for Pensacola, the very city that had condemned Joe to die in prison. Without missing a beat, Joe turned to me, pressed his lips together, and let out a loud "Pff!"

I couldn't help but smile. In that single sound, I imagined thousands of charioteers and horsemen vanishing, swept away by Joe's sheer dismissal of the city's judgment. I laughed out loud and shouted, "Boo-ya!"—feeling, for a moment, the burden of all that had been unjustly imposed on him fall away.

As I would continue to find myself trudging into some dark places in these confinement camps and on death row, I would need Jojo's daringness to dream big. He'd inspire me to hold onto hope because so many others needed whatever little "joy crumbs" we might share.

6

Fathers and Sons

Qwan and I began a practice of sitting together in silence in
those early days of his reintegration back into society. This was
truly one practice of a priest I thought could benefit him. We
had started this shared journey together when he was released
from solitary confinement, and now the outside world was
proving hard to navigate. So, I suggested we quiet ourselves
for just a few minutes at the end of each day. He was game.
It had been two weeks since he'd been released from solitary
confinement, and the difference between the sadness filling
those confinement dorms and the stillness we now sought
was an effort on my part to create a clearing of sorts. The
dorms were a cacophony of noise—clanking chains, screams,
doors slamming, pounding. In that environment, silence was
more of an intruder than a sanctuary. Noise dominated, and
any moment of silence was quickly gulped up by that awful
prison din.

But now, in the quiet space we created, we would sit for a
few minutes in silence, sometimes with a psalm or another
meditative text in front of us. There was no rush, no urgency
to fill the time. It allowed space for whatever thoughts, con-

cerns, or dreams Qwan might have had to surface. Meditation has a way of doing that—clearing the mental clutter so we can listen more to ourselves and to those around us. It invites us to witness the world with a reverence, to see not just the surface, but the living and breathing human ecosystem engulfing us.

John Main, the English Benedictine monk who wrote and taught on Christian meditation, often spoke of how meditation awakens within us a "poverty of spirit." Rather than a lack or emptiness he's speaking of, this is the sudden openness to and awareness of God's desire for us. This kind of intentional silence seems to draw out the desires, even the hurts, that occlude our experience of love. When we're lovingly intentional about silence, it's as if the God who created all out of love surges into our field of awareness—guiding us inch by inch into a world brimming with signs and symbols reminding us how we're all indelibly marked with infinite significance. And when we choose to remain silent with another, we discover more of these brimmings to then share.

In accompanying others, I've discovered how inner silence, the kind cultivated through meditation, makes outward silence more meaningful. It sharpens the senses, making us more attuned to the faces and words around us. There are aspects of life we might otherwise overlook, things we might let pass by unnoticed—like the breath of another soul, quiet expressions of sadness, even while the person we're speaking to may appear jovial. But in the quiet, we hear them, see them. If we listen. It's like we finally become watchful as we trust more in the meaningfulness of existence and the world unfurling all around us.

One late afternoon after several minutes in silence, Qwan dropped one of the saddest lines I've heard: "Oh yeah, I got this call and found out my dad died like two years ago."

Shocked, I said, "Oh no, I am so sorry to hear this, Qwan."

Smiling he simply asked, "Why be sorry? He's just another dead Black man."

Reeling, I sat in a different kind of silence at his words.

Reporting his father's death as a statistic was a way to distance himself from feeling that most hurtful pain: a parent's abandonment. As his father treated him as a throwaway, so too Qwan would shrug him off as a life wasted. His smiling as he spoke this sad news was a way for him to express his rage without feeling that rage. And then, too, Qwan smuggled in the bitter fact of how routinely Black men die ungrieved by our society, as though this was just another death to report.

In stories of family catastrophes, childhood memories adrift, I also heard a yearning to make sense of the unspeakable loss suffered. A loss made even more dark by the shock of violence and the harshness of abject poverty.

In encounters like these with Qwan, as well as others, the pathway to justice might well demand we find solidarity with those who don't count in the eyes of many. But solidarity isn't an untouchable abstraction, it's a movement with and toward. And I realized the gravity of Qwan's oppression was pulling me down, too. We had effectively shared something of ourselves with each other. This isn't lost on me: the extraordinary humility many of these men possess by sharing their pain with me.

Back before we had a house, in those first few months walking with Qwan, I saw the furious swings from one all-or-nothing image to another. Sometimes he called me "Pop," someone he could look up to or even idealize; but in a moment of frustration he could also turn me into an unforgiving and oppressive figure who wanted to own and control him. There might be little warning of the shift, and unless I saw

Qwan suddenly stiffen or hear him coldly say "Sir" to me, I might not even know what had just changed for him or realize we had something we needed to work through together. In those early months it was exceedingly difficult for Qwan to tolerate me being a little good and a little bad.

Qwan had never really learned to see others as fully real people—complex, multifaceted beings capable of being both satisfying and disappointing, loving and frustrating, warm and sometimes remote. Instead, he often saw people as simplified, almost cartoonish figures, divided into extremes with no understanding of the deeper layers that make us who we are. To him, one woman might be a heroine, or someone in need of rescue, or a wicked witch, rejecting and poisoning everyone in her path. A man who was irritable could only be a monstrous abuser with no redeeming qualities, while a prospective employer was either a champion offering salvation or just another person to be wary of. These projections, of course, weren't real. And in the long run, they couldn't hold up.

Anyone who wants to walk alongside someone like Qwan—hell, anyone who wants to walk alongside most people—must understand that they're often seen through the lens of unrealistic projections. We're more likely to be cast as villains or saviors than who we truly are—flawed, but human and capable of growth. But my hunch is this: As time goes on, as the walking together becomes a rhythm of shared space and understanding, idealizations start to fade. The projections fall away, no longer compelling, leaving room for something more authentic—a real relationship, however imperfect.

One of my responsibilities with Qwan was to accompany him to his probation meetings. On one of these trips, something came over Qwan. He put on his headphones and distanced himself from me in the drive over there. The atmosphere suddenly became tense, infused with wordless rage. Slamming the door, Qwan insisted on going to his probation officer alone. So, I stayed in the car, his accidental enemy.

When he returned, Qwan was openly furious: "Man! These police are ruining my life! They want me back in prison. I can't do anything right! They might as well put cuffs back on me and haul my ass back to prison because I'm done."

Locked in a vicious world in which he could only see himself as the helpless target of a sadistic oppressor—and in a way he wasn't wrong—the justice system had rendered him entirely powerless. But still Qwan in this moment was defeated, and he could hold no vision for anything except an awaiting hopelessness and disaster.

We drove to a nearby parking lot where we talked. A complicated picture gradually emerged. Qwan entered an office with a "Florida Department of Corrections" sign on the door. Reminding him and everyone else it was "established in 1868." The sign carried multiple rules, for instance, that no one could enter with a cellphone, no one could bring anything to eat, or, for that matter, to drink, and there were rules on how to behave. While these rules may seem ordinary enough in some settings, Qwan was prepared to see them as demands for humiliating submission. This office quickly became a "prison outpost" where he could be made to feel the power of the state and his own helplessness before it. It was not a bureaucratic office with tedious rules but a dangerous space that evoked bitter and deeply resented feelings of persecution.

To Qwan, I was conveying him to a trap the state of Florida had set for him. Thus, I became part of this hostile system, and he saw me as someone who intended to shame and ruin him.

Qwan's anger toward me caught me off guard. It angered

me. I distinctly recall thinking *ok, so we'll get Qwan a job and then start looking for the next person coming out who might want help from Joseph House.* While this may have been a fleeting thought, it struck me nonetheless. I, too, was ready to give up on this man.

But during the explosion in the parking lot, I started to consider that I would be wrong to take Qwan's attack personally. I was just standing in a long line of people Qwan saw as his persecutors, his destroyers, those who hated him, abandoned him, and would spoil anything good he had going. So, through this explosion, I neither pushed back nor caved in.

I don't recall what I said afterward other than being moved by how poisonous these probation visits were for Qwan. Understanding that was important for our relationship, and just as important was surviving his attack without retaliating against him. In the future, we both tried to anticipate how emotionally brutal these probation visits could be for Qwan and other residents as well. We started trying to change the tone by following those visits with things that were relaxed and enjoyable.

My experience with Qwan at the probation office brought back earlier conversations I had with Maria. She emphasized how necessary it is to enter the private hell of others. Qwan's almost palpable fuming, his slamming the door, and furious outburst against the police and toward me were far more than a frustrated rant. The whole event was a moment of revelation and an invitation to hear Qwan's anguished plea for a secure home.

To sense finally his desire was for me to protect him from these body snatchers, I knew was nothing less than Qwan's plea for someone to be father. The primitive though warranted intensity of emotions evoked by this feared institution of justice revealed why he needed a father: Qwan was himself a scared child. He needed a reliable guide to navigate. Once I could grasp the primal nature with its historical resonance of Qwan's needs and the volatility surrounding them, I began to see the type of community we must establish, a community that could endure such difficult feelings and encounter the hidden needs that fueled them.

It was incumbent upon me then to express my feelings to Qwan—not just emotionally but something fuller, like how I think, what I value, the world I believe we share in. As Maria taught me, all our emotions and thoughts guide us in these interactions, these intercessions, these moments of fullness in confronting someone whose life is being diminished by a justice system that can only see him as an ex-offender.

My revulsion to what I was increasingly perceiving to be a soul-erasing mechanism would strengthen the bonds I hoped to establish between the two of us. This was a moment to hold Qwan's pain and refrain from any plan for intervention. What at times can seem like such a slow process, drops in the barrel of patient listening, can slowly turn to a trusted presence.

It's important to mention, even with my hesitations of anyone interpreting these writings as a reductive trope, many of the men I visit are clearly suffering from a deep sense of disconnection, especially from their fathers. I'm also aware of the irony of a celibate priest from a middle-class home writing this, too. My life has been so far removed from the struggles of poverty and marginalization that many of these men have experienced. But how profoundly hard it has been for so many men to be the fathers they would have wanted to be, given the weight of systemic poverty and a history of social neglect. It's impossible to ignore how larger social and economic forces shape their lives, making it all the more difficult to break cycles of abandonment and loss.

Time and time again, I hear the stories of men living their whole lives in a fog of confusion, shaken by the abandonment of their fathers, their communities, and the very structures that should have supported them.

There's much more to say than this book can cover, but what I know for sure is that in my time with these men, I've often been aware of the need these men have for a reliable, trustworthy presence. It may not always be clear what role I'm supposed to play—maybe a brother, a father, a mentor, or simply someone who shows up. But for many of them, I know, just having someone who shows up, consistently, makes all the difference.

I got the call early one Friday morning.

"Pops, they are going come get me," Qwan said.

What! Who?

"Mr. Matthews, my PO, he called and said, 'Mr. Franklin, get ready, we're bringing you in.'" Qwan spoke in hushed tones, with a not so faint hint of resignation.

For my own sanity at times, I try to imagine these seeming insurmountable forces in fantastical terms, or imagining mythic creatures. Prison has often morphed into the primordial creature Rahab—that multiheaded sea dragon slayed in the myths of some ancient cultures because it resisted creation. It threatened the possibility of goodness.

Creation is God's radical yes. It is the, *I want you to exist!*

Like the wrathful and tyrannical Rahab, the criminal justice system becomes a hostile and aggressive beast that rejects, humiliates, and consumes those wanting new life, those who are trying to escape this perpetual state of destruction. These habits of the state continue to evolve into different, though no less harsh, practices. Probation, often for the poor and destitute, is another way of yanking these men back into state control.

Qwan had gone to a gas station during his restricted time. Walking into a gas station at the wrong time of day would now cost him his freedom. For some this may mean going back to prison for five, ten, twenty years, and for some it has even meant a life sentence. The more I thought about it, the more I realized how Qwan would have easily violated probation in the first few days and weeks if we weren't able to provide reliable transportation, housing, and other material services. For those without these services, violating probation isn't a matter of if, but rather when. It is, as they say, setting someone up to fail.

Qwan would for sure lose his job and his studio apartment. Six months into our accompaniment of Qwan, the work we'd done together would now be undone, derailed, with his time back in jail. Our first reentry success story was a disaster. Two days later I was cleaning out Qwan's apartment.

After Qwan went to jail, I asked Sonya, my friend who had begun this journey of accompanying Qwan from day one of his release, to join me again in our accompaniment of Qwan. We went to Leon County Courthouse in Tallahassee to be there for Qwan as he appeared before the judge for having violated probation. Qwan violated the terms of his probation when—for less than two minutes—he went to a convenience store that was ten feet beyond the invisible boundary of his house arrest. Qwan's unwise and thoughtless trip to the store cost Qwan his job and his apartment and sent him to jail.

It was an ordinary Tuesday as we entered the courthouse that morning. As Sonya and I walked into the courtroom, we felt like we'd entered a time portal.

In our effort to locate Qwan, we looked over to the benches where detainees were awaiting their moment before the judge, and we noticed that all of them were Black and mostly young. As we watched them shuffling over to the judge—all chained together and being escorted by an officer—we heard the rhythm of the chains hitting the ground as to move efficiently they walked in unison, left foot, right foot, then the chain clanked, and it repeated.

I looked over at Sonya and quietly remarked, "Are you seeing what I'm seeing?" Sonya, somewhat stunned, nodded yes.

How was this not a scandal? It felt like the past had broken forth through some wormhole tunnel into our present as we saw chattel slaves making their way before the local magistrates.

Prosecutors, public defenders, and the judge negotiated—or rather bartered—the terms of sentences as the detainees stood silent. These court officials spoke in rapid speech almost at the rate of an auctioneer. At moments it felt like being in an auction as numbers were bantered back and forth. It's not hard to imagine how a fragmented and powerless individual might imbue these towering adults in robes, uniforms, and suits as omnipotent, omniscient, and themselves abased.

The chained individuals were silent, and as I've come to discover, mostly unaware of what their defender and the other court officials discussed as the terms of their sentence were negotiated. It was a mere procedural process to determine the length of stay in our county human warehouses. "Justice" was more a matter of bookkeeping and the question of how long to store this person.

A few days later, I met with Qwan in the county jail.

"I am such a screw-up," Qwan's eye ducts released tears, his face morphed into that of a twelve-year-old boy, afraid and sad.

The Jewish philosopher, Emmanuel Levinas, describes the grounding truth of existence disclosed in the face of the other—the destitute and the impoverished. When we un-cover, or rather, when we are discovered by the demands of the other, we undergo a conversion of sorts that opens us to a new world constituted by the needs of the other.

I sat for a moment in silence just holding eye contact with Qwan.

He told me this from the other side of the window that separates us. And this was the first moment in our nearly six-month journey together that I saw Qwan cry. He mourned what he lost.

"You're not a screw-up," I said. And I meant that. "It was unfortunate, but we'll get through this together."

I felt his disappointment, too. Had my attempts to keep him out of prison failed? Apparently so. I, too, in that mo-ment felt like a screw-up. But seeing him sob in front of me somehow bonded us together even more. We would survive this disappointment together.

As we talked, Qwan told me how bad it was in there. He has secured for himself a weapon under his pillow. Not because of some criminal intent to cut or stab someone but because the prisoner-on-prisoner violence was that bad. Strange how these bulwarks of security are so insecure. Is it because too often these facilities have viewed security as more about those of us on the outside than about those on the inside? With the rate of violence on the inside, you'd think they'd consider the entire institution a resounding failure.

Somehow as we spoke, it was clear both of us were breathing new air here in our conversation. No longer was it about us providing resources and new opportunities for Qwan. In this newfound shared experience of the reentry program crumbling in front of us, we leaned on each other in those uncertain days. I had felt this to be the case from the earliest of days but even more so now because of all that was at stake in this new mission—everything hinged on relationship.

Our mission wasn't merely forward-looking, a way to progress along a certain path and meet goals and prove some type of preplanned view of success, which often is in the eyes of the beholder. Instead, I think of our growth together as the two of us locked together, spiraling deeper and deeper into greater solidarity while the world around us swells and recedes like waves breaking up against a ship.

As I looked at Qwan through the glass, I kept telling him, and myself, we're in this for the long haul. And I meant it.

PART 2

7

The Death House

There was a noticeable difference as I crossed through the various steel gates leading to the main corridor of Death Row and made my way toward "Q Dorm." Usually, there is a raucous atmosphere: guards joking with each other, the steady clanking of chains and other sundry steel sounds, and a commotion in the solitary confinement dorms that often sounds like a full gymnasium. But on this day, there was a sustained hush. Seeing the guards dressed in their Sunday best added to the strangeness.

Today, the state of Florida would execute Darryl Barwick. I was on my way to pray last rites for him.

Before I made my way to Q Dorm, I parked near the administration building of Florida State Prison, remaining in my car to recite the morning office (a series of prayers, mostly from the psalms and prophets of the Hebrew Bible, Catholic priests and those in religious orders pray). These daily readings of lament and the words from oracles struck a chord with my anger as I witnessed the immense pain within the Florida prison system. These codas of despair and disorientation, of hope and unrestrained desire for freedom, seemed to complement the spiritual state of the incarcerated.

As I prayed, I glanced out my windshield and noticed a van had pulled up to the main doors of the building. Staff came and unloaded trays of food and drinks. There would be an office party in advance of that evening's execution. The sadness welling up inside my chest suddenly shifted to anger. How can they gather on the occasion of another's man's killing? Are they not aware that some of us are here to grieve the death of a child of God?

Once I entered the building and sat in the lobby awaiting entrance, I observed two women across from me. They had volunteered to be the state's witnesses of today's execution. Their chatting and giggling further confirmed the spirit of the staff that day as festive. Should I attribute the state witnesses' chattering to some awkward defense mechanism to the events they were soon to observe—or is this some variant of a social tradition long practiced as though some communal execution were celebrated? Probably a little of both.

The echo of the lynching parties of yesteryear seemed to resound here, with townspeople gazing like voyeurs on another man's death. Why has this world bequeathed to us an inextricable tie between festivity and execution?

Descending the stairs into the Q dorm, I landed in the death house. Passing a few guards on my right, and a few suits filling out what appeared to be last minute paperwork in advance of the execution, I finally came to the last of three standard cells where Darryl stood. When I arrived at Darryl's cell, he was making small talk with the officers who would soon escort him to his execution. They had the sports channel on the television and were talking about Florida football. The sight was bizarre. It almost looked staged to appear uneventful. I found this collision, between a sanitized version of everyday and what is ultimate, horrifying.

How strange in this moment Darryl's caretakers, those ordering a meal for him and finally attending to him as if they believe he is a brother, would also be the men accompanying him to his execution.

Darryl was an ordinary looking, mostly bald, middle-aged white man. Here now he was dressed no longer in the standard orange and blue scrubs typical of those on death row. Instead, he wore "the condemned man whites" uniform.

I had gotten to know Darryl in the preceding weeks when visiting and providing spiritual advisement. On the advice of other clergy who accompanied the condemned to their death, I let Darryl guide me as to his needs for his last days. He mostly wanted to talk about the letters he had written to many pen pals, most of whom were nuns. Darryl carried within him this unstated simplicity often expressed by gentleness that struck me as rather constant in his life.

On his last day, Darryl and I spent two hours together. This person whom most know as a man of few words, talked about his siblings and their final round of goodbyes, the upcoming University of Florida football season, and the last few letters he had just sent out. He asked about the men I live with at Joseph House. He asked if one of our residents had gotten the job he applied for.

Pausing between thoughts here and there, he remarked how much he would like for time to slow down. This was not a man ready to die.

Together we prayed a few psalms. He thanked me for spending these last days with him. I thanked him for opening himself to me and told him that I would miss him—I told him I loved him. At this he teared up, looking off to the side, taking in a little bit more of his pending death.

I anointed his forehead and the palms of his hands, as is our custom in this ancient ritual meant to prepare the sick and deathly ill person for their soon transition into eternal life. Today as I smudged "oil of the infirmed" on Darryl's hands and head I saw it as a sign of his dignity and the inestimable value of his body.

He and I prayed in silence as the guards stood watching. A quiet came upon us in the metal and steel—a silence that invited God to be among us. In that moment of silence Darryl and I waded into what seemed the sea of everlastingness. This shared silence is not something I would forget: Standing in silence, holding hands, quietly praying evoked an awareness of a solidarity so deep and fierce the mercilessness of the state could do nothing against it.

Darryl and I shared communion together. We shared the sign of peace as the guards looked on. We belonged to each other. Brothers, both of us.

The clock showed 6 p.m. The horror that had begun to engulf me before entering the viewing room of the death chamber now was drowning me. Darryl had asked if I would attend. I had to be there for him. About twenty others were present, and we were all facing a drawn curtain.

When it lifted, it revealed an overwhelming sanitized whiteness of the execution chamber. It was as though a wave of bleach washed through the room. It took some time before I could make out a form beneath the white sheets on the gurney. Then part of Darryl's recently shaved head and his right arm, pierced with intravenous lines, came into focus.

Darryl's executioner, towering over him, asked, "Inmate Barwick, do you have any final words?"

In all this nightmarish monstrosity, Darryl, though drugged and sedated, managed to speak his final words.

A simple and direct apology: "It's time to apologize to the victim's family, my family. I can't explain why I did what I did."

Darryl was nineteen when he brutally stabbed Rebecca Wendt thirty-seven times to her death in what was initially an attempted robbery. Her death was a brutal killing by a teenager clearly in a state of psychosis.

In my time with him as a spiritual advisor, Darryl stressed he didn't want to add more to his last words when the time came to offer them, so as not to obscure or in any way mollify the sincerity of his apology. After all, he said, "I have had thirty-six years to reflect on what I did."

He was mindful and intentional regarding those last words, telling me he would not ask them to forgive him because that is placing too much of a burden on them.

"Who am I to ask them for forgiveness, it's me who needs to apologize."

Here was a man who preserved his dignity amidst all this hate. His was a dignity solid and immovable.

On the gurney as he offered his last words, he then added, "And another thing I would like to say: The state of Florida needs to show some kind of compassion and kindness for each other with so many kids in prison, there are fourteen- and fifteen-year-olds serving life sentences."

Tears now filled my eyes as I could only think, *You, dear Darryl, have turned this condemnatory moment into a moment pleading for mercy for others.* With these intercessory words, Darryl opened a window to let the prevailing headwinds of heaven into this state-sanctioned hell. He put words to his feeling in that moment, words calling for a more just world.

As he spoke, I also thought of Joe, told by a judge he would die in prison when he was only thirteen. Yet Darryl, just a minute or two before the state would pump poison into his veins, interceded on behalf of all of Florida's incarcerated and orphaned children—this state that leads the country in prosecuting children as adults. In that moment I couldn't help but think how the spirit of Jesus burst forth through the lips of the condemned man. He asked for compassion towards orphans. These were his last words.

He was also, I believe, connecting the dots to his own life, expressing compassion toward the younger version of himself.

The youngest of seven, Darryl was singled out from among his siblings by his father, becoming the recipient of so many beatings. His father beat him with rebar and wood, even as Darryl tried to help his father on a construction site when Darryl was a child.

His father was incarcerated for years before Darryl was born. And at the same prison where Darryl would eventually be executed. Darryl witnessed his father raping his mother multiple times. This young boy, this child, didn't have a chance. His diagnosis of traumatic brain damage isn't surprising, then.

Seated on the first row in the viewing room, I felt a momentary pause in the bleach-white numbness, moved by his ability to call forth these words. Already with sedatives flowing through his veins, this man spoke his convictions. This was a man marked by a surefire love that alights any person receptive to its presence. For just one moment I felt relief, confined there in this chamber of death with the looming presence of a perverse justice inverted to snuff out something good that had begun in this man. And that goodness began well before I visited him. I was simply witnessing all the goodness Darryl possessed. Darryl, in fact, had been designated as an aide by the prison so he could assist a visually impaired man on death row.

My role here, while perhaps viewed by the state as something salvific, was simply accompaniment. This man had already undergone a change years ago, like so many of the men I know on the row. To think of Darryl is to think of a middle-aged man whose task in life was fairly straightforward: He'd pray and read scripture every morning; he'd correspond with friends, most of whom were nuns, all over the world; he'd share his canteen with other men on the row who were experiencing hardship. I'd hear such eulogies from others on death row after his execution.

Darryl would pray the Divine Mercy chaplet every day at 3 p.m., the hour of Jesus's death.

There was something beautiful planted here amid concrete and steel. But in his last hours on Earth, he wrote fiercely to ensure the beauty he created would persist. His legacy was handwritten in these letters, scattered far and wide no doubt to germinate, and one day bloom, in the hearts of those he loved.

To those of us in the viewing room, the executioner read the warrant. The man in the suit then walked to the phone mounted by the door. We couldn't hear the conversation. We presumed it was with the governor's office; the one who retains the power for clemency but never exercises it in favor of the condemned. The French philosopher, Jacques Derrida, notes in his lectures on the death penalty, the act of not giving clemency is to say for all time the condemned is to be unforgiven. In Florida ultimate justice does not forgive. Florida must kill this man no matter who he has become.

Then the man in the suit turned to us, the audience, announcing that the state of Florida would soon execute Darryl Barwick for the murder of Rebecca Wendt.

After Darryl's last words his executioner looked to us and gravely stated "the preparatory phase has ended and now the execution will begin."

At first, I turned to look away, but then turned back in case Darryl looked toward me. In a short few seconds Darryl's eyes rolled back and then settled staring blankly at the ceiling as his chest heaved and left arm twitched. His body, Oh God, twitched and then writhed as though some poisonous snake had slithered under his skin. His eyes remained open throughout his execution.

A few minutes into the execution, the executioner shook Darryl calling his name to determine if he was conscious or not. I looked at the face of the executioner and wondered, does that look also carry a sense of disgust? Is this the look of one who resents having to perform this most cruel role the state has unforgivingly placed upon him?

At this point, I prayed for a quick death, mad that I even have to pray for a quick death for an otherwise healthy and thoughtful man. *I hate this,* I thought to myself. And all its pomp and miserable festivities. It was macabre. I felt as though I was in the audience of a horror stage play.

At 6:14 p.m., after the nurse checked Darryl's pulse, the executioner stated that Florida's sentence of Darryl Barwick was now completed. The curtain closed.

I kept thinking to myself, how evil all this is and then how blasphemous to call this ultimate justice. The feast before this, the giggling, the to-go boxes, everyone wearing their Sunday best. Not to attend a funeral, more like an office celebration for some company milestone or perhaps a going-away party.

I couldn't place things just yet. I didn't want to belong

to those who just extinguished a human life I had come to identify as brother. Not until the van drove back to the admin building when I saw fifty or so folks across from the prison who had gathered for a vigil opposing tonight's execution. Seeing them, with some relief, my eyes watered. Only then could I place this darkness I just underwent.

⫻

A couple of months after Darryl's execution, I celebrated the Memorial Mass of Saint Maria Goretti who died in 1902. Her story is often told as one of moral purity, highlighting how she refused the sexual advances of the nineteen-year-old Alessandro to the point of her death. At just twelve years old, Maria was tragically stabbed fourteen times in an attempted sexual assault that ended her life. Over time, however, an additional, more complex story began to emerge.

Alessandro, after years of living with guilt, had a dream in which Maria appeared to him, offering him fourteen white lilies—one for each stab wound. This act of forgiveness from Maria was seen as a profound sign of grace. Alessandro awoke from the dream with a penitent heart, and he remarked that his dark prison cell, once filled with shame and remorse, had transformed into a garden, now bright with sunlight.

Later Maria Goretti would be canonized a saint, and Alessandro would spend his life after prison as a religious brother, seeking penance for his past.

Some now argue for Alessandro's own canonization.

Alessandro's childhood had been filled with tragedy. His older brother died young after suffering from a severe epileptic seizure, and his mother, after experiencing psychosis, attempted to drown Alessandro in a well when he was just three. She was eventually institutionalized. Alessandro's adolescence, marked by such trauma, was one of misery and despair.

Yet, the same fiery love that transformed Alessandro's heart—he, the man who had violently taken the life of a little girl—was ignited in Darryl too. Alessandro's journey toward repentance led him to ask for forgiveness from Maria's mother. In a profound act of mercy and forgiveness, Maria's mother and Alessandro knelt together at midnight Mass, united in a love that transcended violence, a love that recast the world anew. In that moment, Maria's mother, kneeling side by side with the man who had murdered her daughter, became an icon of heaven's love blossoming here on Earth.

As I celebrated that memorial Mass, I prayed, "Jesus, Maria's savior, bring that same eternal love to us, that one day we might see Darryl as a brother, too."

The words Maria's mother spoke to Alessandro must have left a deep impression on him. No future condemnatory remarks could ever detract from the grace he received in that encounter.

※

Just before Easter, a few weeks before I would accompany Darryl to the death chamber, I was speaking with a couple from my parish. The topic of the death penalty came up. Pam, one of the parishioners, admitted to struggling with the church's opposition to it. She shared the painful story of her high school friend, Karen, who had been murdered while babysitting in West Palm Beach. Pam described the devastating effects Karen's murder had on her and her classmates. For years, no teenager in their area was willing to babysit alone, as the shadow of Karen's death haunted their community. "Karen's death was the defining moment of my high school years," Pam said, her eyes welling with tears. "Forgiveness was hard."

Pam was aware that Duane Owens, the man who murdered Karen, was scheduled to be executed two weeks after Darryl.

After Darryl's death and the Saint Maria Goretti memorial Mass, where I was the celebrant, I saw Pam there. The following day, I received an email from her.

Dear Father Dustin,

Your homily last night about St. Maria Goretti was just beautiful. As you might imagine, St. Maria's story reminds me so much of my childhood friend, Karen Slattery. St. Maria's incredible and inspiring ability to imitate Christ and display such forgiveness has always been very meaningful to me—but the way you spoke about her and how her story contrasts to us today and our society's insistence on vengeance . . . it really brought me so much peace.

Reading Pam's email, I couldn't help but reflect on Rebecca's tragic death and the pain it caused her family, friends, and community. The world often feels darker in the wake of such loss—full of nightmares and grief. I thought of the nameless victims of the men I now accompanied; the ones left behind in the wake of violence. If Alessandro, the man who took Maria's life, could be a saint, what does that say about forgiveness, both given and received?

Reflecting on Maria Goretti's story after meeting with Pam, I realized that offering forgiveness and receiving it are two sides of the same coin—two movements of mercy that restore justice. *True justice, I thought, is the ability to receive forgiveness, to embrace another's love and mercy after an offense. It's a heroic act, allowing someone else's love to fill a space once dominated by shame and misery, transforming it into something like Alessandro's sunlit garden.* This is the reality of redemption unfolding right before our eyes—the way love can turn darkness into light.

I couldn't help but wonder how it must feel when, expecting condemnation, one is instead met with love and kindness.

Today, it is nearly impossible for perpetrators of violent crimes to meet with or even speak to their victims—an appropriate and understandable restriction, given the trauma suffered by victims and their families. But I often find myself wondering how forgiveness can occur in the absence of the kind of encounter Alessandro was able to have with Maria's mother. Maybe, as I've come to believe, in some way I and those who accompany others become the stand-ins for those lost relationships and opportunities for reconciliation. We are God's instruments for reconciliation when we embrace, care for, and accompany our brothers in prison and returning from prison.

Perhaps this is true justice meted out long after their banishment. It's meted out in the everyday life of care and of holding each other responsible. This is the long work of reintegration.

The day of Darryl's execution taught me an unsettling truth about morality and cruelty, and how there may be a perverse connection between the two. As a student of religion and history, I've known that a pure morality and high ideals can be used to justify cruelty. There are plenty of instances in my own tradition when the Catholic Church in the name of perceived natural or moral laws persecuted, tortured, and condemned people who believe differently or appeared outside the created order. How can a supposed moral good cause us to act most cruelly toward another person?

As I left Florida's death house that afternoon where I had witnessed the absurd scene of Darryl's executioners feeding him, joking with him, and preparing him for his lethal injection, it was impossible to tell if this was disguised cruelty, genuine human feeling, or simple-minded denial. What I could tell was that in the name of justice, the state dismissed out of hand the idea of Darryl's redemption, of his being reconciled back into the human family. But perhaps the journey of return to the human family *is* the true fulfillment of justice.

To inject poison into the veins of a fifty-something-year-old man who spent his final hours writing letters to nuns and reminiscing with his siblings was not "justice." I believe true justice would be Darryl's recognition of the grave harm he committed and paying restitution or making amends. There must be punishment, but it should aim at reparation and not simply revenge. There's an inbuilt reparative nature in all of us, something my brothers at Joseph House continue to teach me.

The possibility of justice, true justice, is always creative and redemptive, creating spaces of being restored. Which is why the death penalty is so unjust. Precisely where true justice is most needed, a justice system that practices capital punishment is regressive, justifying the basest instincts, taking away life rather than creating a possibility for new life to emerge.

8

Adoration

Equal Justice Initiative's annual gala was celebrating Joe Sullivan's freedom after twenty-eight years of being incarcerated in Florida. It was a big night to mark this man's life, his endurance, and the incredible work of his EJI family. Later that weekend I joined Maria, EJI's senior social worker, in New York to tour the Metropolitan Museum of Art at the Cloisters.

We ascended the stone steps leading to the hall displaying the Unicorn Tapestries. There was something indescribably wondrous in this display, the sacred images, and relics from the past, with Ennio Morricone's score to *The Mission* piping through the speakers. I felt an immediate cue to be alert to something of great significance.

I had spent most of 2018 jumping about, putting out the small and big fires from Qwan's struggles, making weekly visits in Florida's prison slums, and attending to all the tasks that come with parish life. So, to now pause and enter this cloister felt like ascending to a mountaintop for a breath of alpine air. And to accompany Maria, who had been a fellow pilgrim in those early days, made this moment even more sacred. This was a retreat that felt both restful and inspiring.

What I didn't expect was how cathartic it would be.

First, there were the tapestries dating back to the 1500s in late Medieval Europe. Woven by hand, these tapestries retell the story of Jesus's passion on the cross through the hunt for the unicorn. The story is one of human scapegoating. On the tapestry the unicorn dips its horn into the stream, and thereupon this Christ-like stag is pursued with great hostility. The various tapestries, all depicting the social gathering around a call to bloodshed, was a visualization of how I have experienced the complete brutality inflicted on so many faces and bodies in prison. It is as though the act of entrapment, the poking and jabbing, that follows satisfies some prehistoric need for violence, albeit in these cases state-sanctioned violence. The hunters trap, capture, keep at bay the stag.

The story of the unicorn is an allegorical rendering of Christ's entry into the realm of violence to purify the waters wild creatures drink from. And while so many on death row have in fact caused horrific harm, all of us become implicated by what happens next: the hunt, the capture, the killing. In the narrative tapestry, as the unicorn is executed, a human couple can be seen in one of the tapestries, a lord and lady, whom some interpret as Adam and Eve. In their sorrow they appear to recognize their guilt in the death of this unicorn.

But in that death God becomes that mystical transformative love that regenerates, breaks trauma's cycle, and sets into motion a new power.

Taking in the vibrant colors, the admixture of innocence and guilt, of purity and violence, the tapestries elevate in a narrative moment the faces and situations of many imprisoned prisoners I've seen. In the gallery it is as though the past years of visiting the incarcerated come together in this image. As music from *The Mission* joins the scene in front of me, something in me also connects with the scene of the imprisoned bodies I have witnessed, now rendered present. Each note consecrated our shared work and vision for greater justice and mercy for all those bodies lying underneath the ruins of a failed criminal justice system.

The power of aesthetics isn't how it abstracts and universalizes the particular away from a brief and fleeting reality. Rather, aesthetics elevates the concrete by suggesting there are infinite dimensions waiting to be seen in the ordinary and transient. The iconography of this passion-like story weaves together the transcendent goodness of the stag and the brute-like sadism of its captors into one movement of redemption.

These are the moments when we all must face how interconnected we are: like the grand canvas of the universe and stars and galaxies—all together. *When, oh Lord, will we recognize just how our lives are all wrapped up together?* Reality teaches us how interwoven we all are, how this universe is one massive single organism.

It is a sudden apprehension of divine presence mirroring back-and-forth among all created things. I think of Pierre Teilhard de Chardin, a Jesuit scientist and mystic, in his "Mass on the World," where he meditated on the heart of the world wherein God's presence is glimpsed. Teilhard held closely to the belief God descended into matter (the theological term is kenosis), plunging into the heart of this world, descending to the lowest places. To Teilhard, this is the work of the Incarnation, and it begins the work of redemption—or repair—whether the low place is subatomic, existential, or societal. From what begins as base and basic, reparative work ascends. As it does, it gathers all life to greater fulfillment. When we become conscious of this, we become active adorers. And for Teilhard, we transform the world by what we believe about it.

These tapestries woven five centuries ago connect me to stories woven through history and to the faces I carry with me. Our bondedness comes to me, as strange as it may seem, in the shadows of the confinement dorms. Hearing their cries you hear cries like the one I heard while visiting Santa Rosa when one man screamed "I am a man! I am a man! I am a man!" I hear a man testifying that he shares the heart of this world with each of us. Likely his ancestors screamed the same cry enshackled and deemed three-fifths a man.

Or another man's cry that God hears him. That God ain't abandoned them. I pause in silence, intermingling my prayer with theirs, hoping that just maybe an act of solidarity will hasten our common salvation. Even in these dorms you might witness something transcendent take place that disrupts the loneliness and misery. From seemingly nowhere, a tufted titmouse or Carolina wren, would slip through the concrete walls serenading these men like a winged messenger sent by Yahweh. I remember remarking to one prisoner when one of these birds appeared, how transcendent these birds sound in these concrete fortresses. He replied, "Yeah, we call these our jailbirds." I like to welcome them as God's little messengers serenading the imprisoned, reminding them of a universe vast and wide, reminding them how hope and possibility can escape the tyrannical grip of a system aimed at absolute control.

The more I—the more we—immerse ourselves in a world imbued with transcendence—a world open to mercy and growth—the more we will discover how porous reality is.

While many of the men I visit are not innocent like this unicorn, their plight becomes similar the moment the state and its hunters surround them with swords to enact harm and destruction. For those who set aside the sword, who push past the need for retribution to discover a healing possible through reparation, the story of the tapestry calls us. All of us.

Seeing those tapestries that day taught me how the movement from harm to repair, from offense to redemption, affects us all. We're all caught up in this drama. When we pick up the sword and try to seize control of this drama by insisting some are "the worst," or "the condemned," and have no place with us, we, too, enter the house of the condemned. Condemning, we are condemned, because we are interconnected. Restoring, we are part of what is repaired. I hear echoes of Joe's circle: God takes care of us and we take care of the squirrels—it's a circle. Joe apprehends the same mysteries Teilhard speaks of: that in God all have their being.

The act of adoration for Teilhard unfolds as we become more conscious of God's presence and absence, and only when we lovingly pay attention to human suffering do we discover the one who rises again: almost as if faith is fulfilled when we bring our loving attention to the injustices in our world. Perhaps this is what it means to behold the crucified one: we see God's unending love in the body of a man bearing the wounds of hatred and indifference.

I see this when I see Joe's return home from a stay at the hospital and how he was met in his wheelchair at the front door with big hugs from his brothers at the house. Their care for this crippled man was supreme. The tenderness exchanged between these brothers reminded me of a statement made by the Czech philosopher, priest, psychologist, and theologian Tomáš Halík. He noted that while in the twentieth century following two world wars and multiple acts of genocide, the question of whence cometh evil was posed, now, perhaps, in an age accustomed to evil and violence, we must ask where tenderness and goodness come from?

I sense that enduring divine presence when I see how Joe takes in and absorbs all the love from his brothers. Jonathan Franzen's writes in *The New Yorker* of his encounter with an emperor penguin in Antarctica. While he and his fellow birders approached the emperor penguin carefully so as not to scare it away, the penguin, with otherworldly grace, approached these strange visitors in turn. It then flopped down before them and began gleefully playing with not a care or worry about a predatory threat. Rather than adopting flight mode, this creature became like a child in front of these visiting human beings. The world this penguin dwelled in must be filled with wonder! Instead of inhabiting a world red in tooth and claw, these graced creatures can seemingly imagine a world stretching far beyond retribution. I'm amazed how some emerge from the cruelty of the state with such grace.

Having endured multiple forms of abuse, Joe nevertheless connects deeply with others. This man with a broken body must've dealt with daily aggression and ridicule from staff and prisoners. Now it's almost as though with each touch of tenderness and loving embrace, this man's traumas and abuse are being undone and atoned.

Strange how this journey from death row to building a house for the formerly condemned has taught me about untold depths of redemption. It has taught me how to look for and to adore all the good at work in the subatomic levels of the lives of all these men once condemned. How their lives being restored announces to all of us how enmeshed we all are in this life.

Teilhard believed that science and religion repeatedly teach us just how interrelated we all are, and that our efforts toward justice and peace are replenishing the goodness of the universe. When we focus our energies on building up community life, we are in fact supplying the universe with the nourishment needed for its continual growth.

9

Presence

One day I got a call from Charlotte Morrison, Maria's sister. Charlotte, a senior attorney at the Equal Justice Initiative, had represented Jamie Mills for more than a decade. He was on death row, and the chaplain who had been his spiritual advisor had missed meeting with him several times, and Jamie requested someone else. Charlotte asked me if I could step in, letting me know that Jamie had just been served papers for a death warrant. When Charlotte asked me, I could hear the urgency in her voice and without consulting a calendar, I simply said yes, that I'd show up for Jamie.

In the weeks that followed, I drove back and forth from Tallahassee to Holman to visit Jamie. The long drive twisted through the rural backroads of Blackwater Forest, where the pine trees seemed to stretch endlessly. I passed from the northern reaches of Florida into lower Alabama, the road narrowing the closer I'd get to Atmore, Alabama, where Holman Prison is, Alabama's death row.

The prison had what was called a "visitation park"—nothing more than a large room in what appeared to be the center of the administration wing of the prison. Arriving there to see Jamie, I'd be greeted by his siblings, and then we'd make our way through the gates.

When Jamie and his siblings would gather, you felt their easygoing and long-held love for each other. They had a way about them, a natural ease, that made me feel like I had been with them for years, instead of just a few short visits. There was no pretense, no distance—just a warmth that enveloped me as soon as I arrived at the visitation park. I was not *the priest* here, not someone they had to adjust themselves to. I was simply another member of the circle. Perhaps though, I carried something of the church with me there: a way of saying the love of you all matters to all of heaven and earth.

At one point near the end of our first two-hour visit I told Jamie and his siblings I'd leave early so they could spend more time together. Jamie looked at me and simply said, "Oh, don't worry about that because we already forgot you were even here." We all laughed. I received Jamie's remark as high praise. I was part of gathering, folded into the shared time. Their love was not loud or even sentimental; it didn't demand recognition. It was there, just like the sky above, persistent and vast, casting its Southern gentleness over everything. I realized that this—this ease, this being—was a familial grace no doubt tried over long stretches of time.

His family all wore bright-colored tee-shirts with blue jeans. Jamie wore what seemed to be the typical beige-colored prison jumpsuit with brown work boots. Jamie was fifty, with a mostly grey beard and that same paled white skin tone so many white men had whom I visited on death row. Alabama or Florida.

Jamie was direct—unabashedly so. At one point, nearing the end of one of our visits, he started asking me questions that were kind of like *questions I always wanted to ask a Catholic priest.* He asked, "So, what's up with celibacy? I mean, really, don't you think it's unnatural for a man to be alone? I just can't imagine how difficult it must be. I mean, you know, hell, I'm living a life of forced celibacy in here, but I still don't get the celibacy mandate, Dustin."

I might have felt embarrassed, but the warmheartedness that framed our conversations made Jamie's inquiry on celibacy all the easier to answer. He reminded me of the inquisitive people in my life, those who thrive on equally playful and engaging conversations. It was easy to imagine many more discussions with Jamie. His pleasant smile made his humor the type of easygoingness I can feel at home with. His quippy humor, I interpreted, was a way of bringing me into the sibling circle. It was a rite of passage to enter their shared life. I welcomed that. I don't remember my exact answer to his celibacy question, only that I thought the matter should be revisited by the magisterium. I said that with a smile. I, too, was from Alabama after all. Of course, now I had to explain the magisterium. Quickly I brought the conversation back to something less doctrinal.

Jamie would share his favorite music. Not sure why but I love hearing others share their favorite music. Always have. It brings out their personality like few other topics can. It was clear that his preferred genres were country and Southern rock. He insisted that I must listen to Larry Fleet's song *Where I Find God.* In fact, I think that's how we segued into talking about spirituality. He said, "That song gets my faith."

When I left the prison that day and headed back to Tallahassee, I must have played the song at least ten times—just listening, thinking about Jamie, about who he was. The song captured a love for family and God just being *there*, saturating everything ordinary and loving in life. If this music reflected Jamie's faith, then it was a faith I could subscribe to.

The last two days I spent with Jamie and his family were long. Charlotte, an enfolded member of the family, was also there. We sat together for eight hours each day, the passage of time clicked away.

As the minutes together unfolded, there was something in the space between us—something in the shared conversation and shared stillness at times—that gave the hours weight and meaning. As all of us were seated in plastic stackable chairs around a long rectangular table, it was as though the ordinary passage of time had been suspended, replaced by something larger, more significant. The only time we left our circle of chairs was when one of us stepped out for the bathroom or went to the snack and soda machines.

On the final day, while we prayed for a stay of execution that never came, Jamie slept soundly. His family filled the space with their family lore remembrances, their teasing, as they reminisced about childhood. Those last hours flowed from all our previous visits—siblings taking it easy with one another and with Jamie.

At times, there was that sudden silence, that ominous pending reminder of what was already underway just hung in the air. But even in those moments, Jamie would glance away for a moment, I figured it was his awareness of each moment, looking away to hold those moments tight, a way of embracing those final moments with those he loved. And then as suddenly as he would look away, he would jump back into family dialogue.

Instinctively, I knew it was not my place to speak of God or faith unless Jamie asked. There were moments when I wondered if I should at least offer a prayer for them. But it didn't seem right to impose on their time. I can't explain why—I just knew that this was their time. To impose on such things would not be right.

For his last meal, Jamie simply took a poll from those of us with him about what he should order. Seafood was decided and so Jamie placed the order. When it arrived, it became a family buffet.

As the hour drew near, and the time for his execution came closer, Jamie looked over at me, and asked, "Alright, you want to lead us in prayer, Dustin?"

In moments when all seems lost, when we find ourselves at an impasse, prayer becomes a longing—a desire that the truth of our suffering, the affront to our dignity, might somehow be heard. It is as if we gather the scattered fragments of hope—that once seemed like genuine belief but now seem like nothing more than a fleeting wish—and now offer them to God. It's as though we stand before God, as though much like a child holding up a broken toy to a parent, saying "here, you fix this."

Standing there at Holman Prison, amidst the weight of devastation, our prayer acknowledged the emptiness we felt in that moment. With that conviction, we gathered all the love we could muster and cast it into the realm of a God who listens and hears us.

His family stood around him, including Charlotte, his brother Johnny, Johnny's wife Michelle, his sister Kim, and her husband Robert. We all huddled in a tight circle, each of us praying together.

I prayed only a few words, and then we all prayed the Our Father. By the end, Johnny had begun to weep. His tears for his little brother were uncontained. Then the guards signaled Charlotte to get the phone. She picked it up, and when she shook her head, tears streaming down her face, she turned to Jamie. "Jamie, they've denied us."

Jamie responded immediately: "Okay, Charlotte. You've done everything you can. You've been the best lawyer a man could have."

And then, in an act of tenderness that still comes alive in my heart as I think back to that moment, Jamie pulled Charlotte into his arms. In that moment, I witnessed something that went beyond the anxiety and the looming finality, something transcendent. Jamie, in the face of his own imminent death, was comforting those who loved him most in this life. *And he loved them to the end.*

Before he left, Jamie gave big, warm hugs to each of his family members. He held them for as long as he could, knowing the time was near. Then, I accompanied him to his waiting cell, and from there, to the death chamber.

I have come to believe that this kind of authentic, full-hearted love is in harmony with the divine goodness that we sometimes fail to recognize. No matter who we are or what we've done, we are always so much more than the sum of our actions. In those final moments, Jamie was more—more than the man defined by the state of Alabama, more than the circumstances that brought him here. He was carried, in that space, by the love of his family, and that love, I believe, sustained him in those last moments of his life.

Whether or not specific words of faith were spoken, at times, a wordless presence between us, a communion of silence, and our embraces spoke everything that needed to be said.

When I stood in the waiting cell with Jamie, I noticed the strange, jarring contrast between the gravity, the mournful state, and the irreverence of the world outside. Around us, there were fourteen guards standing just outside, talking loudly, laughing, their faces blank with indifference. The TV blared in the background; the news dominated by reports of Trump's guilty verdict. Jamie glanced at the screen, then turned to me.

"Man," he said quietly, "I hate TVs."

But despite the noise, the laughter, the farce of it all, Jamie wasn't fixated on his own fate. He was at peace with what awaited him, that's what he told me as we sat together in the cell, his thoughts were with his family—his brother Johnny, his sister Kim, and Charlotte. He worried about them, and his mind was consumed with their love for him, and how much he loved them in return.

Jamie also spoke of his sons. He struggled with how he'd leave them with certain matters in life unsettled. I could tell his love for his sons was immense and complex. The uncertainty of how to leave this Earth and know that they are not further harmed. His hesitation here didn't diminish all the love, it only confirmed how much he did love. I suppose that same complexity, a complexity that holds many regrets and still cherishes, abides in each of our hearts.

Rarely do I delve into the news stories or what's available online regarding the cases of those I visit with in prison or accompany at Joseph House. Here, too, with Jamie, it was his person, his heart and those who filled it that mattered most.

Indulging in external accounts—whether case files, news stories, or secondhand narratives—only distracts from my primary task: listening to men tell their own stories. The layers of trauma they carry are already deeply buried beneath formidable defenses, making it difficult enough to uncover their true needs without the interference of outside interpretations.

I remember how profoundly I was impacted when my own therapist refused to let preexisting assessments define me. He had received a battery of psychological evaluations and notes from my previous therapist, yet he dismissed them outright.

During our first session, I asked my therapist if he had received those materials. He nodded. Curious, I pressed further: "What are your thoughts?"

He simply replied, "Oh, I didn't open the package—I put it in the shredder. I'd rather hear from you about yourself. I have no need for anyone else's interpretation."

In that moment, a natural grace settled deep within me. His words were not just an act of trust but an invitation—one that allowed me to exist on my own terms, free from external narratives. I figure I have tried to carry my therapist's approach in how I come to know those I accompany like Jamie.

I was escorted out of the cell and taken outside while the guards prepared Jamie to enter the death chamber. Five minutes passed—maybe a little more—and then I was led back inside, back toward the chamber. This time, as we passed Jamie's now-empty cell, all I could focus on were his boots, neatly placed against the wall.

We entered the chamber, and there lay Jamie, strapped to the cross-shaped gurney, his body covered. He looked at me, shivering, and said with much discomfort, "Dustin, it feels like a meat locker in here."

The cold in the room was immense. In fact, all seemed cold in that moment. It was like we had walked into some portal landing us in some far off very cold planet. It was as though we all had to pass into this alien space, a space unfit for human worth. It felt dystopian.

Standing just a few feet from the foot of the gurney, I began to pray Psalm 23. I prayed it quietly, careful not to let my voice rise, careful not to turn this moment into a hollow ceremony—or into a performance where I simply become a pawn in the deathly mechanisms of the state's execution.

Jamie looked at me with a worried expression and asked, "Where are they, Dustin? Where's my family?"

I turned and noticed the three darkened windows to the viewing rooms. The lights were off in the rooms; I couldn't see any faces. I asked one of the state officials standing to my left which room his family was in. She didn't even glance at me. I turned to the guards flanking Jamie's left and right. Nothing.

I asked, again, quietly, urgently, "Please, ma'am, can you tell him where to look for his family?"

Finally, she glanced in my direction and, with a flick of her hand, motioned to my right. I pointed Jamie toward the window. Jamie's panic seemed to ease as he turned his gaze toward the darkened glass, straining to see. Here, in this death chamber, Jamie still was solely focused on connecting with those he loved. He wouldn't let the state turn this into a mere spectacle.

He spoke his final words: "I love my family. I love my brother and sister. I couldn't ask for anything more." Then, with a small effort, he lifted his hand in a thumbs-up.

For a moment, Jamie looked as if he were bracing himself, preparing for something. He glanced at me, looked back at his family, and with a wink, he seemed to say goodbye.

His breathing became heavier, each labored attempt to draw air weaker than the last. Slowly, his breaths grew more shallow, more distant, until, at last, there was nothing. Jamie was gone.

In those final moments, Jamie had received love from his family, rooting him. That love anchored him, and I believe it gave him strength as he prepared to leave the world.

///

On my way home that night, I thought about space. Strange, I know. About the films *2001: A Space Odyssey* and *Gravity*—where space is unsparing and impersonal, a cold expanse, swallowing everything in its path. But there is a theory in physics that unsettles that idea: entanglement theory. The notion that two subatomic particles can become intimately linked, communicating instantaneously across vast distances, even across light-years.

As I drove back to Tallahassee that night, I couldn't help but think that the silence of space might not be empty at all. What if, instead of being void, that space were to suddenly light up with the communication of all those particles, flashing through the universe like a cosmic web? This was likely an expression of grief and my desperate need for something more that the retributive justice the state of Alabama meted out that night. But even if it was born of a desperate need for more, these needs may also correspond to the indivisible truths underlying our reality—the truth of how we're all connected in this universe.

That night, in Alabama, in the name of the state and its people, Jamie—brother, father, friend—had his life extinguished. And I thought, as I have often thought since: Even though God is always bringing light into the world, always loving us, we, as a society, marshal all our resources to snuff out a human life and in doing this, we sever the bond God created.

10

The Forgotten Coast

When they tell me they have no sense of a future, I hear the echoes of a history of poverty and trauma that so many of the incarcerated experience. History—the events, the lives of those long gone—somehow manages to speak to us in the present, though not always in the ways we expect. For most of my life, I've approached history as something accessible through books and documentaries. But lately, I've heard history speaking through the lives and stories of the incarcerated. The voices of the dead, and the harsh realities that oppressed them, are somehow present in the faces I see. Sometimes, the echoes, the repetition of a cycle of poverty and trauma so deep that it has all but erased the possibility of future-oriented dreams, are striking.

When they speak of lunch or dinner as "chow time," or eating from the "slop," I can't help but think of chattel slavery and the terms still lingering in memory.

When I saw Qwan chained to other Black men, their chains clanking in unison, I could almost hear the echoes of his ancestors—their chains, their suffering, the weight of their history.

There is an opportunity here, a responsibility, to acknowledge the hidden currents of human history concealing decades and decades of social exclusion. The still current harsh realities of incarceration unveil to us the ongoing cycles of poverty and trauma. It's as if each new generation, each new face behind the plexiglass windows in confinement dorms bears the likeness of countless fathers and mothers, opening a sacramental opportunity for me, for us, for White society to atone for past injustices. In the stories of these men, there is the possibility of healing, of confronting the secrets that earlier generations couldn't bear to disclose—or worse, never thought to.

At Joseph House on New Year's Day 2022, Pre and I feasted on our Appalachian meal of fried okra, black-eyed peas, country fried steak, and mashed potatoes. Pre, whom I had met in solitary confinement, was now a resident at Joseph House. Pre had served over twenty years in Florida prisons—ten in solitary confinement. Our table small talk drifted to a memory Pre had of an older prisoner.

"Willy was crazy now. He would at times eat his own flesh. Crazy, right?" He put his fork down, as he recalled Willy. "Man but that dude had this song he'd sing. How'd it go?" Pre asked himself. Then he began to sing Willy's jailhouse song:

> Hambone, Hambone
> grits and eggs.
> Went to the jailhouse,
> fell on my knees.
> The first thing I thought about, my pot of peas:
> my peas half burnt
> my meat half fat.
> Good god almighty couldn't eat that.

Pre laughed in disbelief that he could recall the lyrics.

"Willy Jackson would sing that. He'd been down since he was twelve."

Later I learned later that Willy's song was a new iteration of an ancient African song. Memories are immortal. These songs of oppression, sung repeatedly in a variety of historical moments, bridge past injustices to our present. Memories connect us with our past. Even more importantly they connect us with injustices, historical, personal, or political.

We may be sole individuals, but in our own way we manage to recapitulate the family narrative, much in same way as different actors will play the role of Hamlet or Hamilton in a vastly different way but with the same script. And as in Hamlet, often traumas are passed on in secret. Enmeshed in the web of life are traumas, experiences that continue to climb up the tree of life that we are a part of.

When trauma branches from one generation to the next, if not recognized and confronted, the branch continues the reoccurrences. We know this hard lesson well. If the familial sicknesses aren't acknowledged and faced, the ongoing damage can be catastrophic. This is not only within the branches of family trauma, but also branches of social traumas induced by institutional and political powers onto minority communities.

As I began to research the intertwined histories, I learned that in its post–Civil War economic boom, Florida was on pace to become America's destination spot in the century ahead. Its long coastlands and natural sandy beaches would quickly pass from obscurity to commercial endeavors and tourists' destinations. This state would soon become a kind of curated dreamscape.

Most in Florida are unaware that much of the foundation of its rapid development in the late nineteenth and early twentieth centuries was built by a prison slave-labor class. The infrastructure laying the groundwork for Florida becoming the Sunshine State was literally paved by mostly African American men and boys caught up in the unholy convict leasing system. Sheriffs and judges bartered the lives of thousands of Black men away to industrialists eager to develop the exotic swamplands into a tourist's oasis. It is as though the birth of this state, what we know as "Florida," found its becoming through the controlling and exploitation of its poor, homeless, and mostly incarcerated Black citizens.

Florida's forests are dense and full of life, much of them troublesome for humans. These woods are filled with ticks, sand gnats, and venomous snakes like cottonmouth, dusky pigmy rattlesnake, and the Southern copperhead. You can walk for hours and not see anything but trees, brush, twigs, saw palmetto filling the landscape as well as birds like the red-bellied woodpeckers and swamp sparrows. Unlike the forests elsewhere, these piney woods in North Florida are an oasis for all sorts of biting bugs, not to mention the sudden appearances and disappearances of alligators.

If you listen with your eyes to these longleaf pine trees, some of them ancient and scattered throughout the Apalachicola forest, they might tell stories of a not-so-distant past. You see, these pines carry scars that speak of mistreatment. Trees and swamps, the caverns underneath, and all else that goes into living, breathing ecosystems have a way of recording our history—whether we want it recorded or not. Hiking in these woods winding throughout North Florida's Gulf Coast, you might not know that a larger social history has been recorded here, but you might notice the many vertical scars gouging the interior of these pines. These scars are catface markings on trees once mined for turpentine, telling us of a brutal history of Florida's convict population, a history of torture and death that lies all but forgotten underneath these woods.

As one retired forester in these parts told me, "Father, you peel back enough layers and it's going to get quite ugly for us humans."

Right within these forests is a record of a barbaric form of forced labor, human torture camps, and the brutal treatment of prisoners. These trees bear witness to wounded men who once farmed turpentine from these trees. Gutted and bled out, these crucified pines still stand in our forests and speak of so many prisoners brutalized whose forced labor was used for commercial gain.

Turpentine was in wide use in the late nineteenth and early twentieth centuries for glue, solvents, paint thinner, lamp fuel, and even medicinal use. These forced laborers and other harvesters extracted resin from these pines and began a distilling process. Now these longleaf, tall, and slender pines hold the story in their scars, reminding us however close we remain to the earth, no matter how far we may try to flee into forgetfulness, the scars will continue to hold the memories we'd just as soon forget.

These trees in Florida's forgotten piney woods were extracted for their liquid turpentine as the state of Florida extracted dignity from each forced laborer. In a sordid industry kept mostly hidden, these forests along Florida's coast continue to tell the story to generation after generation.

They tell the story of how overwhelming numbers of Florida's incarcerated—for the most part, Black men arrested for petty crimes—were entrapped in Florida's enormous convict-leasing system.

These prison and forced labor camps were established during the period known as the "New South" when many Southern states sought new ways to create industry in a postwar South. Workers in these camps were mostly Black men who had been arrested under what was known as the Black Codes and later Jim Crow laws. As Florida began the practice of leasing out convicts—many of whom were criminalized for being unemployed, homeless, or incurring debt under a barbaric peonage system—its private industries grew the commercial economies that fostered the idea of the Sunshine State.

One Saturday evening before Sunday Masses, I read one article after another on the history that took place in the woods surrounding my rectory and the homes of most of my parishioners. The next morning, I drove on Highway 98 from Crawfordville to Lanark, winding through the Apalachicola forest. Now, I saw the trees differently as I scanned for the catface markings, a vertical scar near the base of the tree. I thought to myself that these woods must have been mined by Florida's so-called worst. What we have whitewashed in our local history and forgotten, these trees bear witness to countless men made into slaves for the state due partly to their criminality and largely to their being Black. That vast forest history swallowed so many people up—the price of liquid gold turpentine.

With Malachi and Qwan in mind, and countless other poor Black and White men I've come to know in the Florida's prison slums, I sometimes sense for a moment the history, the presence of their ancestors in these woods. Reading the often-hidden histories of these areas, I feel like I'm reading reports of the Panhandle's concentration camps.

One letter documented from that era reads like letters I still receive. Written from a "convict" in Florida's notorious forced labor turpentine camp in Cross City, Florida, August 9, 1921, it reads,

> My dear Mother: I will write you a few lines to let you hear from me. Mother I would have written you before never could get paper to do it. Been down here working in water for four days and now my feet have done got water poison and I aint been able hardly to walk and Willie is gone I dont know where he is. I am sick from wading in this water. I want to leave here and I want you and Ma to try and send me two dollars if you can get it so I can leave from this place, that is the only way that I can get away from here is walk. They will put me in jail so try to get $2.00 for me. I will leave here I am in Taylor [Dixie] county where people is bad. I am sick and my foot is awful sore an no one to help me but you all. So send it this week if you can and let Ma help you get it so Good By-Send it to Cross City, Fla., put my name on it and put it in care of Capt. Brown. I am on his place sick and you must not register the letter you must put the money in the letter if you don't they won't give it to me.

What became of this man? Did he ever see his mother again? Did he remain an indentured servant of the state of Florida? Did he succumb to the harsh realities of wading through Florida's swamps?

Reading this letter, my mind immediately went to multiple letters I've received from prisoners in a similar state of utter desperation. Their lives, even while incarcerated, are often one long stretch of survival. The past is rendered present, and I lament the destruction heaped on so many ensouled bodies in our land.

Often, I'll get a phone call from a prisoner simply wanting to hear the voice of someone that cares. In these moments, it's as though they need to come up for air just for a moment before descending back down into the depths of those murky waters of loneliness.

11

Zeke

I find myself now pulled backward in time, before Joseph House even flickered as a possible thought on my mind. Before entering those shadowed corridors where I met Zeke, who opened my eyes to the grim truths on the inside—not to mention awakened within me a sense of the vast injustices in Florida's penal system.

As I became more attuned to the injustices surrounding me—witnessing human beings subjected to living conditions scarcely fit for animals, enduring punishment through withheld food trays or the cruel use of chemical agents, and men facing beatings from guards out of view of any monitors or cameras—a new narrative began to unfold alongside my awareness.

This emerging narrative was inspired by the resilience and capacity to dream that I witnessed. This narrative opened into my imagining a different social world for these men seemingly tethered to violence and penury, locked behind metal and steel. Even as what took shape around me was human tragedy and a reckoning with a sordid regional history of racism, still what emerged from that tethered life I saw was my own increasing resolve to be a part of creating a sanctuary.

The hill ahead was steep, the challenges were unrelenting, but for those who lived through the unyielding cruelty of Florida's justice system, who find it nearly impossible to abandon the belief that mercy will one day descend, I continue to hold a vision of justice springing forth that recognizes divinity in us all.

Joseph House, with all its peccadillos and messiness, has become the incarnation of that desire. It's a place where healing and belonging have shape. Even if full-blown epic failures unfold, that vision that has stepped into this reality well, I wouldn't trade this or the work it took all of us to get here for the world.

※

One typically hot, humid day in June, I was on my way to P Dorm at Union Correctional Institution in Raiford, Florida, where over three hundred men are housed on death row, and several hundred more are in solitary confinement.

Raiford's summer heat burns bright and harsh. The stifling weight of humid Florida air has no mercy. Between the oppressive heat, the soul-crushing spectacle of these human warehouses, the misery of the captors, and the tedium of their captives stuck in cages, it was a space that could easily make one affirm a godless universe.

In a space inhabited by both guard and prisoner, it shouldn't come as a surprise, as one study concluded, that the average life span of a correctional officer is fifty-nine years old, sixteen years below the national average. Not surprisingly, the United Nations deems confining anyone for more than fifteen days as torture. But there is also a more indirect, more silent form of torture for the men and women who work in these spaces, and regardless of whether they recognize it or not, they are responsible for the well-being of these men in captivity. Guards have called these confinement dorms hell, godforsaken, and miserable.

As I walked on a sidewalk winding by other dorms in a kind of horror film version of an eerie small college campus, I noticed a row of cages—cages you might expect to see at a dog kennel. But instead of dogs, men were pinned in these cages. When I came by, it was their "yard time," and for an hour in these outside cages these young black men could walk a bit, do push-ups or jumping jacks, although most were taking this time to shout to their companions in neighboring cages. Because they were in confinement their recreational time was restricted to one hour before they were sent back into their confinement cells inside.

Suddenly a voice called out from one of these cages: "Hey, Mr. Dustin!"

I looked over and recognized a face from last week's rounds in confinement. It was as though that man was calling my name, saying that ancient verse from Lamentations: *Is it nothing to you who pass by on the way?*

Zeke drew close to the fence as I stopped and looked past the grassy yard separating us. A twenty-two-year-old Black man from Duval County, Zeke stayed in my mind, because the last time I saw him, he was being pinned to the ground under the knees of a correctional officer. Face on the concrete, Zeke was beaming and called out to me, "Hey there, preacher." His was a face and that was a scene I was sure to remember.

Remembering his name, I immediately yelled back. "Hey Zeke!"

Then I saw something I'll never forget. Zeke stared at

me, his shoulders and head dropped. "You remembered my name!" he said.

Like a revelation from on high, I realized then I was in the middle of a sea of forgetfulness. All swamped-up in this unforgiving heat, blistering, beating fever of a world ailing and sick, here he stood, now seen and named.

One way to find our way out of these grim places is to remember that Zeke is a person with a name—to hold onto that and so recover the face before us.

These spaces were created as explicit means to make the guilty know they are being punished. But what if incarceration was ordered ultimately not toward punishment but restoration? How then might we imagine these dorms and facilities? What would it mean for those entrusted with the responsibility as caretakers for the imprisoned to remember their names? Might it lead to a recovery of their own names as well? Their own inestimable value as persons? When you inject mercy into the process of justice, it reveals our shared humanity.

Ten years after Zeke yelled to me, I was now in a familiar schedule of visits. In the intervening years I got to know so many facets of Zeke. Once he had a prisoner companion call me on the phone. I could faintly hear Zeke shouting in the distance from his confinement cell: "Zeke says," the fellow prisoner would tell me, "he misses you and everyone at Joseph House, wait . . . what's that . . . oh, oh, oh, ok, . . . and he says he's coming to you all at Joseph House soon and brings peace . . . oh, yea, . . . he'd like a book on justice if you can?"

He'd call at night and in those calls, I'd hear Zeke passionately remembering that we are all in this together.

Zeke was a child-soldier in Duval County. Forced into the streets before the age of ten, guns and knives were handled as familiarly as spoons and forks. Violent deaths weren't images on a screen, they were seen from his front porch window. He lived with his mother and his five siblings in the poorest of places in Jacksonville. Even at a young age he considered himself the provider for his mom and younger siblings. His role as provider started when he was eight by offering to pump gas for people at the gas station or carrying their grocery bags out to their car. The nature of his work changed when his mom sent him into the streets to bring in more money for their destitute family. Soon the chaos of street life was in him before he could even dream of school or a family of his own.

In our last conversation before his arrival at Joseph House, Zeke and I sat in the office of a classification officer at Suwannee Correctional, with a guard standing by the closed door. In that tense moment, Zeke told me he was going inactive with his gang—not outright leaving, but stepping back. I was crushed. It was as though in an instant my intuition that this wouldn't end well overwhelmed all hope for a peaceful exit from gang life. I tried not to let my disappointment show, even as I wanted to shake him, tell him to snap out of it—to remind him he didn't need these people or the false promises they offered him. But I held back. The guard could take him away at any moment, and this wasn't the time or place to have a deep conversation about leaving behind the Bloods and all they represented.

To belong, or to be affiliated with a gang, especially when you've grown up in an environment marked by instability and insecurity, is a bond that's hard to break. Gangs create spaces of belonging, no matter how violent those spaces may be. They offer a sense of purpose, a way to climb a vast yet unstable hierarchy. To tell Zeke to leave the Bloods behind when he leaves prison would come easily for me. But for him, that affiliation was his way of navigating an incredibly unstable world.

That night, after visiting Zeke, I had a dream. In it, he was free, living at Joseph House. But he was hard to keep track of, darting in and out of sight like a child lost in a mall. I felt the anxiety of trying to keep him within my line of sight, in a paternal kind of role, but he kept slipping away.

I woke with a feeling of unease, and his words and the dream gnawed at me. Eventually, another resident, someone who had successfully moved away from gang life, approached me. He handed me two sheets of paper detailing court fines and fees. Looking at me, he said, "I'm sorry, Father." I read the papers—there were numerous fees, but as I held them closer, I noticed a tear mark running down the page, words or symbols appeared, blurry at first. I'm unsure whose tears they belong to, his or mine. Perhaps they are mine as though I am already grieving the loss of Zeke.

In the dream, my role at Joseph House was in constant flux—sometimes Father, sometimes founder, or to some, Papa-doc. Other times, I was more like a friend, a brother, manager, or a figure of authority. But in this dream, I already felt something parental: the dread of losing Zeke.

I also felt the weight of being left with these fines to pay. The anger I had suppressed earlier that day with Zeke was complex and found its voice in the dream. Zeke had left prison with hefty fees and fines, but they paled in comparison to the debt he owed to the Bloods. His very life seemed to be on the line, a debt that seemed impossible to repay. In the end, these debts pushed him into a place of terrible desperation.

"You don't get it, Father: These people aren't cool with me not producing. I got to pay my debts. I got to be a producer."

This was one of many midnight conversations with Zeke as he sat in my office chair and I on my futon. Now Zeke had been at Joseph House for two months, months filled with celebrations and unexpected achievements like finding a good-paying job with a construction company, like getting his first-ever driver's license and his first bank account. But when he lost his job, things fell apart.

In constant motion, Zeke can be all hip-hop, ready to break into dance without even the slightest prompting. Or all aggressive, fueled by fear. But this night, as Zeke sat in my chair, all that aggression and energy was caught up in fear and despair. It was as though he were stricken with the same pressures that had thrust him on the streets into gang life in the first place.

"I have responsibilities just like you got a responsibility doing your priest thing. I'm a Double OG. [OG—original gangster—is a term of respect. Double OG is one who has been around for a while.] I got to show up. My homies depend on me."

And in my constant attempt to make sense of the roles and responsibilities in the Bloods, I asked, "And what's that, what are they expecting from you?"

Zeke exhaled more air into this already tight space, exasperated by my constant questions. I can't blame him—I am constantly asking him to explain. Because as soon as I think I've finally grasped the intricacies that structure gang hierarchies, it breaks up and vanishes, a dream crossing onto the shores of consciousness.

"I have to collect monthly fees, Father Dustin. Just like you got this diocese and these people are under you."

At this hour, I let it go, with no energy to explain to him that would technically be the role of the bishop.

"I got little bros under me. I have to pull up on them. And then they pay me, and I pay another collector. If I don't pay, that's on me!"

No car. No job, which he lost after he had harsh words for the boss's son. I was thinking, *This is hopeless.* He was too. In a flash it struck me that a potential tragedy was already unraveling in front of us.

Then he pulled out his cell phone to show me another problem he was facing.

"See these texts, I want you to read them so you can know how screwed I am."

Someone belonging to another gang in Jacksonville told Zeke to pay up the $1,000 he owed.

"If I don't pay this, he'll either come for me or he'll start a turf war with my homies in Duval. This is blood money!"

Now injected with the desperation he'd been living with, I didn't know what to do or say. A dreadful mixture of grief and anger gathered in me.

In prison, my relationship with Zeke was much easier. We could talk dreams and goals, faith, and I could listen to his motivational speeches. Out here, all the debts and grievances put at bay during his prison stay just came crashing over him, making everything feel impossible. I felt that impossibility. I also felt his fear kindling into anger directed at me because I couldn't promise everything would be all right. Whatever paternal image had been there faded quickly with every lame attempted solution I offered. I felt trapped too. *This must be what many orphans feel,* I thought, *powerless in the face of the unpredictable whims of a violent and inhospitable world.*

Those fees and fines I saw in the dream before he was

released now seemed prescient, and no less sad. At first, I interpreted those fines and fees as representing a racially biased justice system that screws us both because we at Joseph House pay many of the fines and fees our residents owed. The men feel guilty for me having to pay what the state has dictated is on them. But these other debts, accrued in what seemed like a twisted and violent pyramid scheme of street cults, left us in a heap of trouble with pending violence. All these powerful and unkind structures brewed up a whole terrible mess for us all.

Near midnight, Robert, one of our residents, knocked on my door at Joseph House.

"Yes?" I said, already bracing for something awful. Not an unfamiliar feeling these days.

"Father Dustin, the police are here asking about Zeke."

Lord have mercy. I walked to the living room, eyes still adjusting and now focused on five swat team officers standing by our dining table.

"Are you the pastor here?" one of the officers asked.

"Yes, sorta, yes I am." (Probably not the time to clarify that I'm a Catholic priest, not a Protestant minister.)

"May I speak with you privately?"

"Sure, let's walk to my room."

We entered the same room where three nights previous Zeke, in tears, shared his distress with me. "Zeke Jackson lives here, right?"

"Yes," I responded.

"When was the last time you spoke to him?"

I told him, "Probably three hours ago, just before I went

to sleep. He called to say he was on his way home."

"We have good reason to believe he's been involved in some serious things and may even be dangerous. We are looking for him. Would you call us if he comes home?"

"Sure, yes officer."

And that was it.

A day would follow of me trying to convince Zeke to turn himself in to the police. Trying to avoid any suicide-by-cop situation, I was on the phone with the detective while Zeke was beeping in on the other end. I naively thought I could mediate between the two: on the phone jumping back and forth between them, I felt scared, really scared, for the first time in a while. Frightened for Zeke and scared of what might happen to me and the others at Joseph House as I further inserted myself in this crisis.

That morning, celebrating Mass at the middle school at our parish's school, my mind was full of Zeke's mess. Praying before the gifts of bread and wine, I was overcome by a vision. Before me, Zeke's body lay motionless and bloodied on a street in the southside of Tallahassee. His beautiful, glistening eyes—eyes that had once been full of hope—now seemed to gaze out from the earth itself, frozen in stillness. In that moment, I realized the truth I had been unwilling to see: despair had sealed shut yet another future, fastening Zeke's life permanently to the earth.

But that vision did not come to pass. I breathed, and it slipped off.

Still, standing there, offering the Eucharist, I could not help but look out at the faces before me—these children, innocent and bright-eyed. I thought of Zeke when he was their age, already on the streets, already caught in a world where violence and survival were as integral a part of the universe as gravity itself. As I continued with the Eucharistic prayers, the weight of it all pressing in, tears ran down my face.

The bread offers us all of life's blessings and those little things that bring nourishment, while the cup holds all our suffering and life's disappointments, Teilhard de Chardin captured this in his meditation "The Mass on the World." Both are offered up, not one more than the other, in hopes of being brought into redemption's realm.

In that moment, I could not bring myself to curse the universe, though everything inside me ached to do so. How could I? But I felt an overwhelming sorrow, a deep sense of hatred for the needless violence, for the storms of poverty and desperation that rage against us. And in that sorrow, Zeke's slip from our grasp became all too clear.

Zeke would eventually be sentenced to thirty years in prison, though the state's prosecutor sought a life sentence. Losing Zeke, I was lost myself.

12

Florida's First Seven

The direct lines we draw between cause and effect, as the Scottish philosopher David Hume demonstrated, seldom hit the mark. Yet, as I confronted the tangled web of struggles and bad decisions surrounding men like Zeke, I found myself wondering: Where did this all begin? Was it with the first prisoner in Florida? Whose name sits at the top of such an ignoble list?

I became determined to uncover the history of Florida's prisons, driven by the sense that, in some elusive way, these stories were connected to Zeke, Pre, Joe, Qwan, and others I served. There was something about the lineage of the prison system that seemed to echo in their lives—some hidden thread of history, stretching from the past to the present, tying these men together with the forces that had shaped their fates. In searching for the roots of Florida's prison system, I felt I might discover something illuminative about the lives I was attempting to touch.

///

There's a mystery surrounding Florida's first prisoner. The prison ledger documenting the details of Florida's first prisoners, lists Calvin Williams, age forty. But an eyewitness account of Florida's prison system from the late nineteenth century in the state archives states he was much younger.

What I discovered was that the convict leasing of the turpentine camps arose at the same time in a system of usury, money, and barbarism.

In Florida's convict-leasing camps, J. C. Powell identified Calvin, whom Powell names "Cy Williams," as a "mere pickaninny" (a racially offensive term for a small Black child) in his book *The American Siberia.*

Photos from the state archives of Florida's prisoners show faces in Florida's past that easily could be the many faces I see behind plexiglass windows. Often, I think to myself there's a time portal here. We're all still so intimately connected with these long-ago perished souls.

Johann Baptist Metz, a German Catholic theologian, dedicated his life to reflecting on the Catholic faith in the shadow of the Holocaust. One day, he asked his mother why he had never known that their Bavarian home was just thirty miles from a concentration camp. He wondered how she could have suppressed such knowledge, how she could have lived so close to such horror without acknowledging it. In that question, Metz uncovered a tendency in all of us to block out the evils that surround us.

But Metz's question comes even closer to us in the United States. After all, much is known about how the Nazis drew inspiration from the Black Codes and the Jim Crow laws in shaping their own system of codified racism.

For Metz, the church had long failed to engage with its faith in the context of the world's darkest realities. It had reflected too often in isolation, detached from the brutal history that had shaped humanity's suffering. Metz considered the memory of Christ's passion, death, and resurrection a dangerous one, because it compels us to confront the world's injustices. It calls us not only to remember the past but to act in the present for those who are oppressed, who are without hope, and who seem doomed to failure.

If not recognized and confronted, trauma moves virally from one generation to the next. The damage our looking away has done has been catastrophic.

Our soul is inseparable from the universe from which we've emerged. Zeke's universe, tragically, was filled up with a destructive chaos that even I couldn't escape, because generations had allowed the systems of trauma to continue. I was facing a chaos not only of one set of events, but events upon events, debts upon debt, and it tightened its grip on us both.

Around the time of Zeke's arrest, my researching of Florida's prisons intensified. It felt like an act of care, as though I needed to know more about the institution that had wreaked so much havoc. I found myself wondering about the legacy of this institution that, while on the surface seems necessary for social order and punishment, recorded abuse upon abuse against the poor and imprisoned.

During an orientation at a prison one morning, I found myself staring off in a kind of tedium. My eyes happened to fall on the badge of a correctional officer. It was the emblem of the Florida Department of Corrections, marked with the letters "FDOC" and the date "Est. 1868." At first, my mind was elsewhere, and I glanced over it without much thought. But then, something hit me—*1868*. The Florida Department of Corrections had been established only three years after the end of the Civil War. This meant it was founded at a time when thousands of freedmen were struggling to forge their newfound freedom in the aftermath of emancipation.

What did it mean that this institution was born so soon after the war? What kind of systems were being put into place for those newly freed? I delved into the history of Florida's prisons with more intensity, which eventually led me to the museum at the Apalachicola Arsenal. Located near the back of a state hospital complex, this modest red-brick building is all that remains of Florida's first prison complex. It was here that the state's carceral system took root and began to grow.

Accompanied by Pete Cowdrey, a parishioner and local historian, we were led through the small museum by an elderly curator from Tallahassee. We were soon standing before a table, where the last artifacts of Florida's first prison were laid out. The curator gently opened a large, tattered ledger to the first page, revealing the names of Florida's first two hundred prisoners. She turned to the first entry: *Calvin Williams.*

We read aloud the details of his incarceration:

Calvin Williams / Male / 40 years / Height 5'6" / Eyes: Black / Hair: Black / Complexion: Black / Town: Lake City / Occupation: Laborer / When: November 21, 1868 / Where: Columbia Co / By Whom (the Judge): Thomas T. Long / Term: One Year / Crime: Larceny / Received: December 31, 1868.

Six others were also listed on that first page: Amos Adams, Joseph Adams, James Monroe, Thomas Stewart, Henry Arnold, and Squire Jones. Of these seven, six were Black. These were Florida's first prisoners, marking the beginning of a system that would become a cornerstone of racialized oppression in the name of justice.

As Pete and I studied the ledger, the curator shared with us a striking story. A correctional officer had found this very book a few years ago, discarding it in the trash. Then realizing its potential significance, he retrieved it and brought it to the museum. It was now a relic from a time of great historical import for anyone interested in the Reconstruction Era in Florida and its legacy on Florida's carceral system.

During Lent of 2022, Calvin Williams's name began to echo through my thoughts with increasing frequency. His name began to intertwine with the name of Zeke. Calvin's story became more than just an echo of the past—it felt like a living connection to the present.

Through Lent and beyond I continued to research, learning that Florida wasn't historically unique in the aftermath of the Civil War. Like other former Confederate states, Florida restructured its carceral system not just as a means of punishment but as part of a broader effort to control the newly freed Black population. Like other Southern states, Florida enacted laws designed to criminalize Black men, sentencing them to long prison terms and forced labor for both petty and serious crimes. In 1868, with the establishment of Florida's first prison in Chattahoochee, the seeds of state-sponsored cruelty and exploitation took root in Florida's soil and would eventually evolve into the convict leasing system, turpentine horror camps, massive solitary confinement camps, and the death house.

J. C. Powell, who himself was a former convict-camp captain, wrote in *The American Siberia*, about the brutal conditions of Florida's convict-leasing camps, where prisoners were treated as little more than expendable laborers. But it was in his description of the first prison, with its "horror's den" and the use of solitary confinement—"shutting them up in a close box cell without ventilation or light"—that the true extent of this cruelty became clear.

This shadow history moved from horrifying to more horrifying. One early Saturday morning I found a YouTube video about the Apalachicola Arsenal. The video offered a brief timeline of the building's history: from its beginnings as an arsenal manufacturing weapons during the Seminole Wars, to its role as a Confederate training camp, to its later use by the Freedmen's Bureau, and finally, in 1868, its transformation into Florida's first prison.

The very space that had once been intended to welcome and assist newly freed Black citizens in their transition to independence had been repurposed, almost overnight, into a site of imprisonment for Black laborers. Florida's first prison was born from a place once symbolizing freedom, now an institution entrapping and exploiting the very people it was meant to protect.

On December 31, 1868, New Year's Eve, Florida's first prisoners, including young Calvin Williams, were transported by the prison wagon and entered the same building that housed the Freedmen's Bureau just months earlier.

I don't believe we're fated by our past. Nor do I believe we're some blank slate unconnected with what came before us. Yes, the treacheries of the past break into the present. And those hazards created by our ancestors may ensnare us into the seemingly eternal cycles of violence. But that's not everything.

At Mass I am instructed only to offer both the bread and the wine, blessings, labors, and disappointments, to the infinite creator of Zeke, me, and all those who came before us.

All the violence and tragedies can't suppress the world's potentialities. As a Catholic, the incarnation is for me a radical embrace of this world. It teaches us to discover the indestructible good among and within us, to neither ignore the disappointments nor let them subdue the glory encompassing us.

This gathering, this communion, moves forward not by grand gestures but by the quiet, unseen power that arises when we embrace one another with love. It is through our mutual care, our shared acts of mercy, that we make space for transformation. Each day, as I count my own transgressions and my small acts of mercy, I come to realize that these, too—seemingly insignificant—are part of the larger tapestry of the world's redemption. In this, God, I sense, discovers me. Discovers all of us. In this vast, ailing world, it is love, tender regard for the faces and bodies of others, even those dead and buried in obscurity, that continues to resist the tug of despair.

13

Mothers and Sons

It was the day after Thanksgiving, our first at Joseph House. A quiet afternoon settled over us as we slept off the excesses of the previous day's indulgence. The house was still. We were all nursing our postfeast fatigue.

I was sitting in the living room when Amos, our newest resident, introduced me to his mother and her husband. They had come to Tallahassee to visit him before returning to Marianna, a small town an hour west of the capital. Amos had been released from a prison in rural North Florida about three weeks earlier. Now, he was staying with us at Joseph House, working to rebuild his life and reintegrate into a world that had, in many ways, moved on without him.

We spoke, sharing stories of the dishes we'd consumed over the past twenty-four hours—turkey, stuffing, mashed potatoes, and pies, too many pies—each of us recounting our culinary triumphs as if we'd somehow achieved something monumental by simply eating our way through the holiday. It felt good to laugh together. But then, as if on cue, the tone shifted.

Amos's mother, her eyes moistening, spoke with a depth of pain that pulled us all in. She began to recount the years of separation, the ache of his absence from her life. Her words, at first tentative, began to unravel the years of hurt, of missed moments, and of a son who, for so long, had been cast off far away from home. The pleasantness of the holiday conversation faded into the background, replaced by the raw truth of her grief and perhaps even unconscious anger.

It was as though the room held its breath, the gravity of her sorrow sinking into the quiet. We had all been so focused on the feast, the indulgence of the season, but in that moment, the conversation turned into something far more meaningful. The joy of the holiday was tempered by the pain of the separation—the years Amos had spent locked away, and the years his mother had spent waiting for him to return.

In that shift, I found myself reflecting on the layers of this moment: the joy of reuniting; the pain of separation; and the difficult, tender process of healing the wounds that had been left in the wake of Amos's absence. The anger that she too felt at being abandoned. It was a reminder that the work of rebuilding a life doesn't just happen in a day, or even a month. It's a long, slow journey—one that winds through the past, through old wounds, and into the meandering work of repair. These meanderings over time have built our house into a home.

We had picked up Amos two weeks before Thanksgiving. It was an early Thursday morning when Rachel, our social work intern from Florida State University, and I drove out to Mayo Correctional, on the far eastern edge of Florida's Panhandle. As we made our way through the winding roads, Rachel, young and full of energy, wore a smile as bright as the midday sun, and her warmth could match the best of Southern hospitality. She had a passion for Broadway and could effortlessly drop pop culture tidbits into any conversation.

Over the years in this ministry, I've come to have a deep respect for social workers and the often thankless work they do for the most marginalized in our communities. I've been blessed to work alongside tireless advocates like Rachel who go to great lengths to ensure that those most vulnerable aren't forgotten. Rachel exemplifies the best of social work, and in many ways, she was groomed for this role from an early age. Her mom made sure Rachel and her siblings watched *Dead Man Walking* many times over. Rachel knows that film frame by frame—an early education, perhaps, in the complexities of justice and mercy.

On that morning drive, Rachel kept me awake and alert, talking nonstop about everything from criminal justice reform to the latest drama on *The Bachelorette*, to hometown church gossip, and, of course, the game plan for Amos's first week at Joseph House after a thirty-year prison sentence. Thirty years for second-degree murder—a robbery gone wrong, with a fatal outcome. When we arrived at the prison parking lot, an officer came over to inform us that there had been an incident at the prison, and Amos's release would be delayed.

Finally, we saw him—Amos, standing there with all his worldly belongings in one small sack, dressed in clothes Rachel had chosen for him based on his interests. We always make it a point to get to know the men we're welcoming home as best we can—learning their clothing sizes, favorite colors, and favorite meals in advance so that we can offer them a sense of dignity the moment they walk through our doors.

As we drove, Amos told us about the night before—about

a gang fight and stabbing that had erupted in the prison. He hadn't slept a wink. Rachel, ever the conversationalist, immediately began chatting with him, fast and furious, keeping the conversation light, trying to ease his mind. A master social worker at work.

A few days later, Amos would share with a group at Joseph House that his first night with us had been the most peaceful sleep he'd had in thirty years. The constant cacophony of prison life—slamming doors, clanking chains, rattling keys, the sound of toilets flushing, shouting, officers reprimanding prisoners, voices crackling over loudspeakers, and the occasional scream of terror—had left its mark. For Amos, like for so many others, the noise was unrelenting, filling every waking moment.

Often, when I leave a prison, I'll sit in the quiet of my car in the parking lot for a few moments, letting the noise fall away from me, bit by bit. I imagine, for someone like Amos, that noise must seep deep into the bones. Buying him a suitable mattress, fresh bed linens in his favorite color, is more than just a practical need—it feels like an act of social justice. It's a small but important gesture of restoration.

※

Amos's mother, Wilma, talked in the manner of someone profoundly wronged who has had no access to remedy, and she instantly showed us a previously unseen depth to her son's life and his presence in this world by declaring: "My son was taken from me at an early age! I haven't had a son in twenty-seven years. I mean I had a son, I had Amos, but did I really have him? He wasn't around, you know. He wasn't there to be with me. He wasn't around when I needed him."

In this complaint about the long absence of someone who was loved and needed, his mother redefined Amos as someone with infinite worth, a worth that could only be experienced in how much he was missed.

Wilma introduced her son to us with a quiet but profound understanding, as the sole witness to a story that might otherwise have been missed. She reminded us that Amos, sitting here with us, should not be seen merely as a released prisoner spending the holiday with new friends. Her words revealed something deeper: her pain over his long absence had been a silent testament to the value of his presence now. Amos was not just a man in transition; he was a beloved son, a member of a family.

Amos is a small-boned, slender man whose manner in this world is deferential and polite. Rattling from within this bald and brown-eyed man is a bluesy baritone voice that sounds forth words of wisdom as though formed by experience measured over long years under extreme adversity. He's an old soul, in a middle-aged man's body. Often, I'd wonder how he managed to preserve his soul in the thirty years he spent in the state's control.

Amos was charged and convicted of second-degree murder. At nineteen, Amos, after already being caught up in the juvenile justice system much like Zeke, took part in a bank robbery when someone from his gang shot and killed a man. Amos was a member of this group, not the gunman, but nevertheless was sentenced to thirty years in prison.

Blood and death weren't new to Amos, long ago in his adolescence he had already seen people shot, knifed, die in front of him. So because the state considered Amos an adult at nineteen, this teenager was taken away from his family and exiled into the prison system. Amos is a short, slender Black man now forty-nine years old.

With his baritone voice, he tells me, "Now, now Father Dustin, I tell you, prison is hell from the moment you get up to the moment you go to sleep. You think I'm kidding but I ain't."

Amos would speak this same sentiment in multiple different versions over the nine months I got to know him through Joseph House. His story, like most, was a story of constant survival under the tyranny of concrete, steel, and suspicious eyes looking at him, from either guards or fellow prisoners. There were moments when I'd look at Amos, consider the thirty years he did in prison, and see that the weariness had taken a toll on his body and mind.

Listening to Amos and his mother talk, the thought occurred that in the span of three weeks we had come to piece together stitch by stitch the fabric of this man's life: his family connections, his interests, his virtues, his quirks, his work ethic, his humor, and his unquestionable devotion to sports in general and the Miami Hurricanes in particular.

Before this, however, all we were shown about Amos was the grim image posted on Florida's Department of Corrections webpage, which features all 100,000 of Florida's incarcerated. This despoiled image reduced Amos to nothing but a mugshot. The image presented him to the world as though he had no life story other than the felonies listed below his name, whether he had tattoos, possible aliases, or other identifiable features you might want to know. The way these headshots are featured it's almost like a snapshot of a trapped animal so that just in case it escapes, someone might identify it and return the creature to its rightful owner.

But here in our living room, his familial connections came alive. Like seeing the intricate tapestry of family suddenly unfurled before me, the intimate, meaningful human realities that matter most to all of us surfaced as his mother spoke of her son lovingly though with regret. Once again, I was reminded just how dehumanizing today's criminal justice system is, this time illuminated by the flood of tenderness expressed through the relationship between a mother and her son. Their caress alone was a testament to this man's dignity.

14

Circle Home

My wishes for community had imposed a hefty price to be paid now that these ideals had proven unrealistic. In those early months at Joseph House, I couldn't have imagined anyone in the house community returning to prison life. But this happened a mere seven months into our new fledgling community on Bradford Road.

And while I still believe we are all mysteriously interconnected, it doesn't necessarily make living together easier.

Two months into Amos's stay, it was clear he and Quintin, our house manager, were not getting along. Amos increasingly was becoming erratic, some volunteers sensed he was high as his speech became belligerent. Now on edge around Amos, Quintin expected a prison-like brawl to erupt in the house.

As house manager our first year, Quintin had a quiet, unassuming presence—exactly what we needed for the role. Having completed a lengthy sentence, Quintin arrived at Joseph House the year before. Quintin would often share long, reflective stories about his time in Florida's prisons and the lessons he had learned along the way.

When he first visited Joseph House for an informal interview, Quintin expressed a desire to pursue his education full time. "Plant yourself here," I told him, "and we'll make sure you have the time to study." This was a lifelong dream for Quintin—one that had seemed irredeemably interrupted when he had committed his crime. When you get to know someone like Quintin, a man who had spent years in Florida's prison system, and you sense the deep longing in his soul for something more, you find a way to make that dream work.

That first couple of months at Joseph House had gone remarkably well. We hosted large weekly community events, with people from all walks of life coming together to help create a beautiful, clean space for our guests. Visitors often remarked on the warmth and hospitality they felt as they stepped through the doors. Quintin, meanwhile, was thriving—he was making straight As in school. Amos was working full time, and Joe kept our daily social events running smoothly.

Then, one Sunday night, I received a call from Quintin. The police had been by Joseph House the day before, looking for Amos. My heart sank.

Quintin's voice was grave as he reported, "They said a mother called the police, saying her daughter had stayed the night with Amos at the house."

From the beginning, we had decided that overnight guests were not a good idea for multiple reasons—chief among them, the potential for unnecessary drama among the residents. And that's exactly what followed.

The tension between Amos and Quintin quickly escalated. In Quintin's eyes, Amos had broken the rules, and in Amos's eyes, Quintin had betrayed him. Once suspicion and resentment began to fester, there was no returning to any semblance of normal. The once calm and harmonious atmosphere in the house now felt charged with hostility.

Quintin, defensive and frustrated, began to feel the weight of his responsibility as house manager more than ever. I preached peace, but Quintin had to live in a house that was teetering on the brink of conflict. It became a zero-sum situation—Quintin's position as manager was now a threat to Amos's stay, and vice versa. Both men began to fall back on prison terminology and behavior. It was as though the incident had transported them both back into the harsh, defensive culture of prison. I could feel the tension in the air, the kind of energy that often precedes violence.

But what I didn't know at the time was the immense pressure Amos was under. Only after this crisis did I learn that Amos had been threatened by former gang associates—he, like Zeke, had to pay his debts or face dire consequences. He must have spent sleepless nights waiting for the sound of gunshots or the knock on the door. This was around the time Amos had reconnected with former gang members and was once again drowning in the debts of his past life.

Amos talked about how there are two kinds of people in prison: those who *do* prison and those who *prison* does. The former are those who resist the system, becoming hardened and tough, while the latter are broken down, passive, and compliant. Amos, it seemed, was the former, and Quintin, his words suggested, the latter. Was this Amos's way of venting the anxiety that came from the very real threats of violence hanging over him? I could certainly see that in hindsight.

I remember the feeling of prison creeping into the house—it's hard to describe, but it's a sensation you begin to recognize after a while. It's a kind of coldness, an absence of human warmth that fills the space. It's like that liquid metal, mimetic polyalloy to be exact, which allowed the robotic villain to shapeshift into other people in the *Terminator* film. (Or that's how I visualize it.)

One night, Quintin called me. He was standing outside, looking back at the house, and he said he felt afraid of it. He associated the house with the same fear and tension he had experienced in prison. It had become, in his mind, a dangerous place, a symbol of everything he had fought so hard to escape.

"I hadn't made the accomplishments I have to end back up in prison," he told me.

Quintin's words carried the weight of someone who had come too far to let fear and survival instincts drag him back into the system. His sense of safety, or rather the absence of it, was the key to his freedom. When men like Quintin feel safe, they flourish. When they feel threatened, panic sets in, and they make decisions driven by fear rather than reason.

One night, we gathered as a house to discuss the escalating conflict between Quintin and Amos. Accusations flew, and the word "snitch" was dropped. There is no more damning label in the prison world. To be called a "snitch" is to be marked for life—betrayal, punishment, and ostracism follow. In prison, it can be a death sentence.

At that moment, I knew we had reached a low point. Unfortunately, I tried to intervene with a kind of idealism that was more about my own need for resolution than a practical understanding of the situation. I thought if we could just talk it out, if only they could see each other as brothers, we could avoid the collapse of their relationship. But I had no experience with conflict resolution, and I was no mediator. And this was no Camp David moment.

Leaving that conversation, I felt the fragile nature of the peace we had tried to broker. It wasn't real. It was more about my need to restore some idealized sense of unity—one that never truly existed in the first place. My desire to fix things blinded me to the deeper, more visceral fears both Quintin and Amos were carrying. Both were afraid. Amos feared the violence from his old gang associates, knowing they could strike at any moment. Quintin feared Amos—his escalating anxiety had turned into a survival instinct, and he could see no way out except to leave.

The thread of safety that had once bound us all together in that house had snapped. Now it was back to survival mode. Quintin was convinced Amos was a ticking time bomb, capable of exploding at any moment. He feared he would be forced to defend himself, and that would land him back in prison. For his part, Amos was certain Quintin had betrayed him, and now was persecuting him with new, stricter rules. What neither Quintin nor I knew was that Amos was facing a much darker threat—one that had haunted him from his past.

It all spiraled to the point where Quintin felt he had no choice but to leave. Roger, one of our core community members, called to tell me he had put Quintin up in a hotel room for a week. It was a hard decision, but I couldn't blame him. He felt the house had become unsafe, and once the label of "snitch" was dropped, there was no coming back from it. The trust was gone. The fear had taken over.

And so, Quintin left. It was a loss, a painful one for all of us, but it was also a reminder of how fragile the bonds of safety and trust are. In the absence of those, survival becomes the only thing that matters.

We helped transition Amos into his own apartment. It was heartbreaking to tell Amos, who in many respects had made good strides in reintegration, that he could no longer stay at Joseph House. This of course made Amos more dependent on precisely the people who were jeopardizing his future. But if our mission was to prevent homelessness and recidivism, I couldn't just tell him to leave. It was up to us to build some bridge for Amos from our house to another place. We did that. But still Quintin wasn't ready to return. So there I was, lying on the couch, staring at the ceiling and thinking life would be easier if all of this would . . . go away. I knew I wasn't skilled with managing relationships and enforcing rules.

As I lay on the living room sofa that night in a house now nearly empty, I thought how it only took a few short months for Joseph House to fail. A rivalry that spiraled downward in a matter of days had now led to Quintin's departure and me having to ask Amos to leave. It was only Joe and me at the house. Even Joe was talking of going to live with his family. I had failed. Was it naiveté thinking we'd created a haven for those retuning?

The smoldering ashes of a community hardly held embers that night on Bradford Road. And the world, in all its complexity, paid no mind to our dreams. Had I expected too much? Should we become more schooled by reality and embrace this mission becoming like other halfway houses, rather than attempting to create and establish an ongoing community of men who make their way to us?

Prayer in these moments, those quiet little spells that come upon us when dreams can't even take flight, somehow kept me grounded in this world. Enduring this dark night was more than I could bear, hoping as I did for a loving, peaceful community where bonds are created with those the state of Florida calls, "the worst of the worst."

From this point on, I decided, I'd have to make allowances

for imperfections, disappointments—and complete disasters. The ongoing challenge for anyone directing or leading such a community is to balance the understanding of disappointments when they come with a realistic hopefulness that good may continue to develop, if unevenly.

How I think of it now after this mess-up is that my mission is to endure faithfully in love. This is not a head-in-clouds love, but reality-tested, earthy, ambivalent love that is unrushed and unimpressed with progress as well as unafraid of regressions. I think of it as a postapocalyptic faith in humanity after a nuclear fallout has occurred: Sure, we can blow everything to smithereens, but that does not change the fact we still need each other.

To me, risk is that singular portion of love for this world that believes in change. Risk is that power that makes what isn't *be*. Risk is what we do when we let love escape from the enclosed spaces of our heart. Risk may even entail leaving behind the fantasy of an idealized "we're all getting along" with its repressions and the silencing of our concerns and living in the reality that holds hope. Reality was this: All those years imprisoned in the violent unpredictable prison world and it was still casting its spells on Amos and Quintin. For a community to emerge, it would require my letting go of these fantasies of everyone-gets-along and replacing those fantasies with whatever primal unity could be attained.

Sadly, it was only a matter of a few months after Amos's departure from Joseph House that he was arrested. A few months after his arrest, Amos called me collect from a federal jail in Florida.

"Father Dustin," he said, "I've pled out, so I can tell you what happened—all of it."

After being arrested and charged with a drug sale, Amos was looking at a lengthy sentence.

"You remember when I told you I ran into someone at the bus station the day I had gone to pick up a bus pass for work, and I was scared?"

I recalled Amos being apprehensive about taking the bus and that he tried to avoid some bus stops.

"I do."

"Well, that was the day someone from the Bloods saw me, and they reminded me of my debts to the gang."

"They told me if I didn't pay up then they would come and put bullets in my home, in Joseph House. Father, they knew where I lived."

There's no question that gangs are the bloodiest of cults.

Amos had been in prison for a thirty-year sentence for second-degree murder. His robbery was a gang act. He told me that his participation in robberies began when he joined the Bloods. What appears to be a record of a basic criminal act related to money and ending in bloodshed is a larger story of a man's life largely defined by poverty and desperation.

For those familiar with communities focused on restorative justice, the "circles process" will be familiar. It's a staple of these communities and designed to provide a way for people to share stories of harm and healing in communities marked by violence. It is a method that acknowledges the fractured relationships between people and the need to restore those bonds.

Quintin, Joe, Chandra, our circle keeper, and I sat together in the circle. These circles are frequently used in restorative justice practices so that we learn to hear more from one another. Each person is allowed air space to speak on their feelings, complaints, needs, whatever they may wish to share with others. They are structured so any issues of harm may be repaired and relationships restored. In our little community they were structured times for sharing any challenges, complaints, needs, or hopes one may want to share. In this way I viewed them more as healing circles wherein one experiences a felt sense of community support.

Quintin began by recounting an incident from earlier in the day.

"I came up to Father Dustin," he said, his gaze distant, "and asked him where the cookies were—the ones that were on top of the refrigerator. And he told me he threw them in the trash."

There was a subtle tremor in Quintin's voice as he spoke. I could sense the storm of emotions brewing beneath the surface.

"Father Dustin," he continued, now pointing at me, shaking his head, "he told me if I wanted them, I could get them out of the trash and eat them." Quintin continued, "I don't understand why he would tell me to eat trash," he said, his voice thick with disbelief.

I was stunned. Here I was, a priest who nourishes others with communion, yet Quintin believed I was telling him to eat from the trash. His words cut deeper than I expected.

Quintin, still struggling with two conflicting images of me, saw me as both a man of compassion and now as someone commanding him to eat trash. The two could not coexist in his mind.

In circles like this, in order for people to have a chance to speak—uninterrupted—an item, sometimes a "talking stick" or another object, is handed to them. When they have the talking piece, everyone else's role is to only listen. So, by the time the talking piece came to me, I had already felt the sting of Quintin's words. Too defensively I said, "Quintin, I'm sorry you perceived that, but I had just tossed the cookies into the trash, and they were still in their package. Since they were at the top of the trash, I figured you could take them if you wanted."

Quintin shook his head in disbelief. He wasn't buying it.

When the talking piece returned to him, he said, "I don't know why Father Dustin, a priest—a man of God—would just tell me to eat trash. I mean, those are words that could get someone hurt in prison. That's low."

Another tide of defensiveness, now mixed with anger rose in me, even as I also began to wonder was he right? Was I acting cruelly? Did I not care if he ate from the trash? His questioning my integrity now created confusion in me.

In that moment I realized the word that kept returning. I wasn't just a priest in this moment—I was a father. Not just an honorific, not just a religious role, "Father" carried the weight of paternal responsibility. What *father* meant was that I needed to hear him, understand his trouble, and find a way to assure him that I didn't wish to poison him—either literally or metaphorically.

In all of us, there lingers an echo of a small child's anxiety of being born into a world full of contradictory feelings: the warmth of nurturing and the painful pangs of hunger. The fear of losing the good, of being abandoned, is a primal fear that we carry into adulthood. As adults, we don't "lose" our memory of being that child, and so we may experience this paranoia when a trusted friend disappoints us or when someone we admire acts in a way that betrays our expectations. In that instant, we may be inclined to respond in defensiveness (as I did) or in fear, splitting that person into "all-bad," interpreting from one behavior an implication of an entire past of that behavior, debasement, manipulation, or whatever. In our pain, we shut them out, coldly and decisively.

Now the talking piece came back to me. "I never told you to eat trash. I just thought you could take the cookies if you wanted. I'm sorry if I wasn't clear."

We cycled through a few more rounds, but by now, it was clear something deeper was happening: Was Quintin really asking me, *Can you nurture me? Are you safe?* Could I be the figure of care and stability he needed, or was I, in his eyes, just another unreliable source of pain?

I thought of the many men who have told me they had, at some point, eaten food from the trash in prison out of sheer hunger, or witnessed others do the same. In that moment, I recalled the furious passage in the book of Isaiah where the prophet condemns Babylon for its treatment of exiled Israel— a people stripped of their dignity and forced to subsist on the barest remnants of life.

Here, in our circle, we were grappling with the same primal struggle for dignity and nourishment, searching, desperately, for a way to be heard.

Internally, I said, *Dear God, Am I just another in a long line of superiors who have proven cruel, one more figure to wield power over them, to reinforce their isolation? I feel the weight of their anger, the distrust thick in the air.* The tension was now palpable, as if the whole room were holding its breath, caught in an endless loop of miscommunication and resentment.

Amid this confusion and hurt, there is also something

remarkable in human nature—the capacity for integration. Over time, we talk, we circle, and we circle back. In those circling backs, we learn to reconcile the good and the bad, to accept that both can occupy the same space. The need to split the world into opposites, into "all-good" or "all-bad," begins to fade. The persecutors—whether external or internal—disappear, and the energy once spent on constant vigilance diminishes. Life becomes less threatening.

Often in the process I'd think to myself how much Amos would have benefited from these circles. It may not have saved him from the trap of the gang debts, but it may have created more opportunities for connecting with us, allowing us to carry some of his anxieties.

The process of repair is a slow rebuilding of trust and connection. It's a crucial part of the reentry experience—learning to live with the tension of what has been broken and what can be made whole again.

Over time, I began to understand the high stakes of not just keeping the kitchen orderly but of understanding how one flip comment from me could be the language of prison and diminishment for another. And Quintin began to understand that I wasn't telling him to "eat trash," I was simply trying to keep the kitchen orderly, navigating the delicate balance of food and sanitation in a shared space. And both of us began to understand that we were, in a sense, speaking two different languages to each other.

Looking back, that circle marked a pivotal turning point in our relationship. It was one of those rare moments where we could trace the cycles of hurt and healing, of anxious concerns and desires for destruction, only to return to tenderness and regard. These cycles of repair, no matter how messy or imperfect, expand our capacity to love and to be loved.

///

Amos, though separated now by barbed wire fences and steel gates, held to a circle of his own making. He'd call me. Ask how Joe and Quintin were doing. Laughing when I'd share with him Joe's latest escapades. We'd talk football. We'd also discuss what had happened. As Amos told me, the trouble with former gang associates began two months after his release. He was already working for a local roofing company and doing well until Amos ran into the former gang associate at the bus stop. An old friend of his helped him pay his gang debts but only if he'd make a few drug runs in exchange. It was an easy out with incredibly high stakes. To pay off a few debts, Amos would offer his life. He didn't want to. And he was not thinking criminally. It was fear for his life and the sheer distress brought on by destitution that led him back onto the streets.

I knew how much he dreaded these bus rides, but I didn't know why. Once again, he was trapped. And now he was being threatened, given the choice to either enter the criminal underworld or to pay with his life—and possibly the lives of those he lived with. The threats were real. His options limited.

Amos's predicament post–Joseph House is tragically emblematic of so many of our returning citizens. Crimes brought on by poverty. Crimes brought on by unlivable situations. If I'd have known how precarious his situation was, I would have worked hard to ensure that Wilma's son wouldn't ever have had to ride the bus in Leon County again. Once a former gang member sees you, you're on the run. Amos wasn't free when he walked out of those gates. His gang debts chained him to his past; often these gangs can be as unforgiving as the justice system.

15

Purgatorio

In my dream, my therapist and I were standing by a window peering out into the vastness of outer space, discussing the nature of transcendence, which I stressed had incredible importance. As we looked through the window, emerging from the dark skies of space, was the planet Mars. What began as a small red dot in the deep dark distance grew as it seemed to come toward us. As the red planet neared, so did its rich and beautiful complexity, as though moving from a global view to a zoom-in view as we began to see finely detailed, three-dimensional landscapes on the planet. In this strange dream universe of mine, Mars's orbital path brought the planet right alongside our observational window. Whoosh! And then it sailed right by us.

In my dream, we eventually sat back down, resuming our session in our proper roles of therapist and patient. At this point, as we discussed the nature of transcendence, we clarified how it isn't something to be explained. And together we wondered at how something can appear and be seen whooshing past us and yet elude explanation.

As one who tries to pay attention to dreams, I brought it into therapy. We discussed what was at stake with *transcendence* in the dream. We went into depth on the symbol of Mars. My therapist pressed for other possible interpretations. Something in line with the interpretation of Mars in the traditions of Western civilization. Yes, of course, Mars, the God of war.

"It seems to me," my therapist said, "with Joseph House you have gone to great lengths to create an environment, perhaps even one with order and beauty, so that moods, needs, experiences can freely emerge." He paused, looking at me for a moment. Then he said, "There's a mystery and transcendence involved in the work of resisting easy solutions, keeping at bay neat and easy moralisms from stifling the interior needs of residents. This is something you've contended with in the past, no?"

I nodded yes, affirming this has been a point of contention in the past.

He continued, "Here perhaps the surprise of Mars's orbital path drawing near is what you are trying to do, allowing the internal wars that entangle the residents of Joseph House to become visible while surrounded with care that is as reliable and durable as the solar system."

Amazed at the wonder contained in this bizarre dream, I followed what my therapist just proposed: "There's an elegance to this universe honoring mysteries contained within. If we step back, I think, and lower our own defense mechanisms, defenses that project ideals of moral purity or the supposed purity of some social science paradigm, then we open that observational space to encounter the hidden tempests within, wrath and anger that have suppressed their more ancient needs for love and respect."

As he spoke, I recalled Maria Morrison's repeated refrain

in this journey of accompaniment that we should "let their needs guide us; their conflicts too."

Three years after picking up Qwan at the bus station, we picked up José in an open field across the street from Florida State Prison. He was finishing a lengthy sentence, the last three years of which were spent in solitary confinement. Like so many, he'd leave his dungeon cell and head straight for the free world.

Anyone's transition from the pitch-darkness of the inferno to a sunlit purgatory will be bewildering with amazement, as those first days and months leaving prison may overwhelm one on their new voyage. The sheer temporality of being alive and moving about in one's own way and one's own space can induce ambivalent feelings for those once lost in a prison world.

The terraces of Dante's purgatory move round and round the mountain like habits, resurfacing again and again and reminding us just how difficult it is to let the past go. It's not difficult to understand how one may become jaded following a long-term traumatic experience or how those familial ghosts linger as a constant reminder of the people whose love failed us. These purgative terraces are apt metaphors for what those who emerge from prison often encounter leaving the hellish timelessness of prison life to enter the very here and now that presses on us in free life.

It was a midsummer morning when the DOC van pulled up beside us. Rachel, our social worker at Joseph House, and I immediately got out of the car. José, a man of Puerto Rican heritage in his mid-thirties wearing a kufi, jumped out of the van with a sack over his shoulder. He was pale with that familiar yellowish tint of those emerging from solitary confinement.

"Hello there!" José greeted us.

In those early days with us José revealed his encyclopedic knowledge. He could recite verbatim Einstein's Theory of Relativity. He knew America's presidents (and vice presidents), listing them in chronological order. He could quote passages from both the Qur'an as well as the Bible. I was confident he would opt for the university track, perhaps discovering a love for history or science. But once he saw our carpenter start on the building project of our gazebo, it was clear José longed to work with his hands, preferring as he did the outdoors.

José had striking features, hair wild with curls, thin as a rail, but I'd be willing to bet every ounce was muscle. And no one should take his skeletal features as a sign of weakness. Wiry like a UFC fighter, you sensed he could easily go fist to fist with a heavyweight champion. José was also quick to anger. Any slight sign of something off, of something not quite right—like a slight inconsistency in my proposed timeline for going to the store—held the potential for a match striking tinder within José.

Often José's frustration was more or less appropriately expressed through a "C'mon Father Dustin, you can't be that forgetful." But there were times when José could turn to quick fury, venting without much restraint. In moments like that, it was hard for me to remain Yoda-like. Sometimes I would give in and fight back. *The world is burning, and I better do something.* Anger can be contagious. While I always maintain a nonviolent stance, when all that rage is aimed at me for perceived slights, it's difficult to not respond.

At these times, I felt as if José has handed his rage to me, putting it into me, as though tossing a grenade at me, saying, "Here, let's see how you handle this!" Who can fail but emerge from Rahab and not bring some of Rahab's prison viciousness into the house. Sometimes there's a feeling I have of, *So here we go again!*

One cold night right after Christmas, while typing some late-night emails, José knocked on my door.

"Father Dustin," he started, and I could already hear grievance in his tone. I opened the door to both present and ancient wrongs.

"Don't you know, Father, one fuck-up on these time sheets and I can go back to prison because these numbers are not adding up, and *they* will violate me."

Standing angrily over me, José held out his community service hours log sheet, as I sat at my computer desk.

"Playing with the courts is no joke, dammmn!"

How could it be lost on me that in that moment of course José would be anxious, since we turn in these monthly time sheets to the Leon County Courthouse—the same place that sent him off to prison for a seven-year bid.

"I hear you, so why do you think these numbers are off?" I said, hoping to work this through with José, which was perhaps nothing more than a stalling tactic.

"Because November was already turned in and these sheets are for December, but they also include November in it, y'all be playing with my life here."

With a dead cold stare, he looked me in the eyes, effectively communicating contempt at us for not taking him seriously.

The precariousness of the situation was not reassuring.

What I heard him say was, "You aren't trustworthy, and you don't care if I go to prison." I could see I was in a line of people who had let him down.

Those dates rendered him powerless. He needed clarity and order. And he wanted it from me. He didn't see himself as having power. José, like others, didn't sense he had the power to navigate around this world, power he perceived I had. That sense was soon projected onto me and attack is enacted. Fear begets fury. And disorder can feel like imprisonment.

Relationship isn't a means to an end; relationship is the end. I try to remember in moments like this. Together we ascend through these terraces while almost ritualistically recircling through passages from confusion and rage to conversation and resolution.

What I didn't think about in those moments was that he sat in county jail for over a year before going to prison. No mother or father visiting him. No one appearing to care. He spat and cursed at the prosecutor, and no one there thought to listen to see what he might be saying. And now as he faced me from the doorway, it was as though I was the recipient of that rage, I was all those people who never listened to the pain he held.

"José," I said, "I need you to turn down the volume."

Nope. Epithets were slung fast and furious at me and then he walked away into his bedroom. Minutes passed, and I thought to myself, *Just let the wrath-cycle run its course.*

As I then sat, staring blankly at the computer monitor and the unfinished email, I thought, *What is history saying here? When would someone verbally go on the offense with the slightest hint of an inconsistency?* But if we care about origins and destinies, and the journey between the two, then we also care to understand how these histories inform our realities. It is only love that leads us away from hastily tossing peoples' actions into the bad behavior box—toward gaining insight into those interior dark caves where ancient hieroglyphics tell us a story.

José came into adulthood in gang life: Creeds of bloodshed, survival, and alliances formed through pacts of death; this was his community. His father and mother disappeared, leaving in their absence a child looking for mentors. The storminess of a frustrated youth, crippled by orphanhood, outlined his story and reminded me to read those severe mood swings at perceived neglect not as pathological but as an invitation to listen—better—to the story he was telling me.

In one of my first lengthy one-on-one conversations with José, he narrated for me the story of his initiation, a story filled with violence, neglect, and regret.

"Father Dustin, I do not want to go back to that life. But it's hard. Those streets are what I know. And I don't see how I can possibly make it."

Sitting outside smoking, his manner was mild but his fear palpable. The gravitational pull of the streets is a powerful force. José might just go back.

When he opened up about his childhood, I saw it as a courageous act, maybe a work of love. It was as though José was saying, come and walk with me as I share with you. But getting to the point where he would confide and want me to accompany him required time and shared experience. That included our driving to the bank together, creating shopping lists together, doing store runs together to pick up meds for one another. Most especially it required attention, and sometimes I miss what is there to be seen.

However, he told me one story that captured so many of the childhood horrors I heard over the years from countless incarcerated men. I listened in a way then that has me still listening now as the story echoes through me. José's story qualified, in my estimation, as a primal scene: a life-altering event for a child.

One summer Sunday evening, right at dusk, while seated at our community table near two large windows looking out into our garden, José told me of a recurring nightmare that recently resurfaced. I waited, knowing that in his time and way, he would share what he wanted to say. Those who patiently accompany folks through enough small and ordinary tasks know that then the mysteries of the human soul will surface like a sea creature from the depths, coming up for air.

At the time we spoke, José had been out for a month, straight from solitary confinement at Florida State Prison to Joseph House.

"I've been having the same dream again. I used to get these dreams in prison. There are these demons," he said. "They be coming out from the woods in the back of the home I grew up in when I was a child."

These ominous creatures haunted his sleep for years.

I asked him to talk more about this house and those woods. José then gave a kind of dead stare far off into oblivion, lost in a time warp, I suppose.

"Well, yeah, there were these woods back there and that's where my pets were buried." José was sitting with me at the dining room table, but it was almost like he was alone. He said his grandfather used to punish him when bad reports were being delivered from his school.

"Yeah, you know things could get pretty bad," he began.

Then he said, "So when I got home my pop would give me the gun and tell me to shoot one of my dogs. And there I'd grab the dog and shoot it point-blank, right in the head. And then I'd have to go and bury them in the woods." Finally, he looked at me. "These were my dogs, my pets, Father Dustin."

It was maybe the worst thing I've ever heard about a childhood with all the love taken out of it, all the pain put into it.

"José, this is awful. Dear God, I'm sorry."

"Nah, don't be, that's when I became a man," he said. Manhood born of violence. He told me how after one of these slayings he was a sulking thirteen-year-old, walking and whimpering, when he came up to one of the tough older kids in the neighborhood. The man told him to stop being a pussy and stop crying. After that encounter José started his initiation into a brutal career in gang life.

I can't help thinking what violence he must have wanted, quite naturally, to inflict on his pop for making him carry out that soul-emptying slaying of his pups. Perhaps those phantoms emerged from the woods in these night terrors as the rage he wanted to visit on his pop but turned instead on others in his gang life.

But now, he was making a break from life in the streets. Working long hours, building his own business, and most importantly, learning gradually how to become a pretty good father to his children. I watched him do all those things. I know it's slow work, redemption, and it never goes in a straight line.

Our needs are dangerous. They remind us we may well be disappointed. Worse, they might lead us to unforeseen and risky transformations. Asking for, facing what we need with all the treachery and impossibility of the process may sometimes feel as if we are trying to defy gravity.

That cold December night, trying to understand his concerns, I walked up to his door and knocked. Opening the door, he looked at me, and I waited for one . . . two . . . three full seconds. And then I saw it, a smile broke through. He said, "I love you, Father Dustin."

Where does tenderness and goodness come from? I'll always ask that question. It stuns me every time.

It's as though tenderness says, "I love you. Now, can we talk this out together?" The need for a mutual back and forth, a reciprocity like the levers and wheels of a machine turning and pulling, creating a dynamic together generating power. That evening, I understood that it's a pulling at something together—collaboration—that José needed. It's power, a voice, a say in the matter that he needed. To feel like we're working with him, listening to him. Not minimizing his casework—a signal that said to him, yet again, there's neglect from those looking after his needs.

But when we wait for each other, hold still for a little while with the other in mind, well, that's one powerful binding force of love in this life. Love draws all things together. It instills in us the call to be responsible to each other. I knew, yes, probably tomorrow we'd go through it again, but that is also how I know love endures. It muddles its way in fits and starts.

There was no "I'm sorry" or "I'm all bad" or "You're bad too," to seek to rebalance the social world at Joseph House. That's not reparative conversation. Conflict doesn't require our confessions of guilt. In that set of moments, there wasn't any forced repentance. Neither of us apologized. We simply acknowledged our love and care for each other and stated our concerns. Yes, it's rare, but when love like this is exchanged, things are atoned, freed, released, repaired. When love like this is exchanged, personal history is revisited and acknowledged.

And . . . that's some theologically sophisticated stuff enfolded into seemingly simple exchanges of our shared humanity.

Each of us holds remarkable power to enter another's orbit, to be attentive to the other's world. This can become the chance to behold new worlds rich with extraordinary meaning. It is as though the human universe is structured around the possibilities of relatedness, such that each of us, with sudden sight, beholds the other: The word becomes flesh and *dwells* among us. When we dwell with each other, forging bonds of belonging, each of us becomes even more intelligible to the other.

Maria often tells me about the scientific literature she finds on incarcerated people, relaying how they are referred to almost exclusively as "offenders" or "prisoners" or "criminals." The language of the literature uses terms like "assessing risk" and "dangerousness," about the need to address "criminal thinking," and how a "treatment-resistant population" was scarcely what she witnessed among those incarcerated men she met. She said she didn't see indications of persistent dangerousness; nor did she hear what sounded like criminal thinking. What she did encounter, she said, was something very different: a frequent deep longing for connection and learning. Now, in real time, that's what I've been experiencing with Qwan and José.

Joe, José, and I strolled along the seashore at Saint George Island. We were there to celebrate our dear brother Quintin's wedding to Anastasia. A few parishioners opened their beach house community for this celebration.

José pushed Joe in his beach-friendly wheelchair. I looked at them and thought, *My God, here's a former gang member now caring for his handicapped brother.* I held this image of these two men together alongside an awareness of all the bickering and shouting that goes on between them, too. And . . . that moment was still glorious.

The work of accompaniment embraces the reality—perhaps even sometimes the contradiction—of the coexistence of love and hate, care and neglect. None of this diminishes the sheer glory of such moments as these, of Joe and José, of the waves breaking gently against the shore; of gulls and pelicans carrying on overhead, and the sky above gradually emptying itself into deep blue.

We penitents walked the beach, and it felt as though eternity had interrupted the ordinary. The eternal and the temporal intertwined, heaven and Earth coincide, and eternity's horizon appears precisely at the same moment it disappears. Perhaps this is how love here on Earth enlivens heaven above. Who knows?

PART 3

16

Heralds of Zion

Right around Christmastime, after Joseph House brothers went to sleep, the house was quiet, and the tree lights turned off, I bumped into Joe at the Keurig. Both of us were looking for that late night fix of caffeine.

"I thought you were asleep, Joe," I said, seeing he was still wearing his sleepy face.

"I was. But I'm awake now." Joe looked up at me from his wheelchair, rubbing his eyes, "Ready for the night, round two!" Then he said, "Hey, I had this dream, right. We were at Walmart."

"You and I were at Walmart? I thought I was banned from Walmart trips." The guys at Joseph House recently voiced their dismay with having me join them for the weekly Walmart trips. Apparently, I don't like shopping. I'm more of a buy-and-go kind of guy.

"Oh no, not you. I was with Pre and Chad. So, I was trying on this shirt, right? And this stranger, I don't know who he was, he was from prison, he came up and started saying mean things to me." Then Joe dramatically shook his finger as he said, "He was saying he was gonna do this to me and that to me."

Then Joe did what he always does. Getting to the good part in the story, he paused as a slow rumble of internal laughter begins quaking before it erupts, shaking him all over and taking over with an explosive howl of guttural joy.

Joe regained his composure, saying, "So Pre looked at that man and said, oh no you don't." Joe shook his finger again. "He starts pointing to this. . . ." There it comes again, eyes shut, mouth open wide, belly laugh just rolls out.

"What did he do Joe?" At that point I really wanted to know.

"Pre is a silver-back gorilla, he stacked!" Joe said flexing his muscles. He's right, Pre is not one fella I'd want to get in a scuffle with.

"Pre comes up and says you got a problem with him then you got a problem with me. He starts beating his breast." Joe flexed, indicating the muscular strength of Pre.

Now the mean stranger was in flight. Joe's recounting this victorious dream gratified me beyond words because I knew how often Joe was ridiculed and teased while in prison. How many times did guards and other prisoners make fun of him? He came there as a child in a world of adult strangers. Well, now he had Pre and other brothers to protect him. He had a safe place, with loving bonds forged in slow time.

Hearing his dream, I became more convinced than ever that only community can heal our deepest fractures.

※

"It's been years since I got under a Christmas tree."

José nearly dove under our well-adorned Christmas tree, which stood tall, its green branches heavy with twinkling lights and an abundance of gifts as those in the house exchanged presents with one another. For two of our brothers, what made this Christmas so special was that it was their first in years. For one, this was his first Christmas celebration in twenty-two years. Both approached the holiday with unrestrained excitement, their childlike joy lighting up the room as they fully embraced the celebration.

The tree, an eight-foot centerpiece in our living room, radiated warmth and magic. The lights shimmered like a modern-day deity, casting a soft glow over the gifts that surrounded its base. Christmas songs played softly through the TV, and the atmosphere quickly became festive as the house members gathered, each eager to unwrap the surprises waiting for them.

As the men tore off the wrapping paper, it felt as though they were unearthing long-held wishes, sharing them with the rest of us. I couldn't help but think to myself, *This moment—this is Zion.* The thoughtfulness of their gift-giving to each other created a conscious expression of love and care.

There are moments when Zion feels realized, when everything seems to drip with the sweetness of grace, when tenderness and excitement flow freely between us. This Christmas morning had all the markers of Zion—a world, even if only temporarily, reimagined as a place where each of us truly belongs to the other.

That night, something remarkable happened. Without any instruction or encouragement, each man bought a gift that seemed so perfectly suited to the recipient's personality. It was as if the joy of Christmas created a spontaneous bond among them that, growing over time, found a kind of overflow in our living room. It felt like a family had finally taken root.

Joe bought José a winter hat and gloves, knowing that José loved working outdoors. Joe must have seen him tinkering on his car during those rare cold Tallahassee nights and thought, *José needs some winter gear.* Joe noticed José. Pre bought José three jumbo cans of tuna—an unusual gift, perhaps, but you would have thought he had gifted him a Super Nintendo by the way José held the cans high, proudly displaying them as if they were trophies. This too was freedom: the freedom to be loved.

Chad bought me an ink pen set, knowing I wanted to do some more writing. José gave me a travel mug, which was perfect for the long drives I often made between parishes, the house, and all my daily errands.

As I watched them open their gifts, laughter and cheerful nods filling the room, I couldn't help but reflect on the depths of each man's past. My mind drifted to each of their lows—the violence, the hardships—that could have easily stripped them of the ability to experience the simple joys we were sharing that night. I thought of the faces one had seen pulverized at chow time in jail or the time one of them heard a body hit the ground after being pushed off the third floor in the solitary confinement dorm. From the stories they told me over time, I recalled the blood that had once stained the floor of a cell after a man was killed by his bunkmate or the life that was taken in the yard simply because someone was gay. I thought of the correctional officer who had once threatened to take one of them outside, casually stating he'd "killed and buried four niggers and would do the same again."

All that brutality, all that bloodshed, and yet here they were—sharing a life together. Just months ago, these men had been strangers to one another. This was justice in its truest sense: repairing harm, creating a space where they could belong. All I had to do was put up a tree, a tree donated by a few parishioners, and watch as these men poured their hearts into building something new, even if just for one night.

And in that moment, I couldn't help but think, *Where do tenderness and goodness come from?*

In a few short days, the tree would be tossed to the curb, the gifts discarded or forgotten, and perhaps old rivalries and bickering would resurface, but none of that could diminish the power of this moment. In the same way the stars burn brightly in the night sky, only to slowly fade and collapse into darkness, we are reminded that the meaning of life lies in its fleeting moments. To appreciate this life, to truly understand it, we might learn to embrace its brevity and vulnerability.

The realization that justice is possible, that we've created something beautiful together, filled me with a sense of delight. And while I've had to unlearn the belief that such joyous togetherness could ever fully solve our problems, on that Christmas Eve, we celebrated a common home, a space where each of us belonged. And maybe, for that night, that was enough.

I have come to hear what I like to think of as new hymns of deliverance sung by those still in exile. Joe and José, like those ancient Israelites returning from Babylonian captivity, were trudging through new territory, having survived traumatic experiences brought on by their capture and exile; these refugees were trying to recover those ancient promises of reconciliation that God had spoken through the prophets. Like Florida's imprisoned orphans, these Israelites were emerging from the throes of confusion and despondency as we read in Isaiah: *a people robbed and plundered all of them trapped in holes and hidden in prison*s. And yet now crowded around this festive joyous tree, redemption's song is faintly being sung. I knew it took at times great strides to make possible something like this, and I hoped perhaps foolishly to increase as many chances as possible for it to be repeated. I am not sure what is supposed to happen after a miracle, what follows when the eternal invades the temporal, but I have to imagine Lazarus died again. Who knows?

To begin the slow work of loving requires my own capacity to be loved. To see and be seen, from this, reciprocity begins. This meant I became a brother. And there's a lot involved in becoming a brother. If I was going to extend a hand of friendship to them, acknowledging their history, I, too, had to extend that same compassion to myself. They held a claim on me. I was seen by them, too. They welcomed me into their space as much as I have welcomed them.

17

Night Healing

We found ourselves preparing to move into our second home—right next door to Joseph House. Amid the buzz of excitement, we were planning to host numerous community members while simultaneously remodeling the space to accommodate three new brothers later that summer. It had been four years since we moved into our first home.

The community felt a collective sense of anticipation, but there was an undercurrent of responsibility among a few of us, aware of the significance of welcoming three brothers transitioning from Santa Rosa Prison. That summer, we reflected on healing and what Joseph House aspired to be: a therapeutic community grounded in safety, proximity, and patience. This period of transition allowed me the space to delve deeper into the philosophy that underpinned our mission.

Enter Murdina, our new social worker, affectionately called the "OG social worker" by the brothers. In her late sixties, Murdina was a veteran in social work. At first, her genuine warmth and friendly New Zealand accent disarms, but those working with her quickly learned she could be relentless when advocating for the dignity of those grappling with housing, addiction, and the profound traumas of incarceration. Murdina had a way of placing the person front and center, and if necessary, she wielded a colorful vocabulary to challenge institutional approaches that prioritized bottom lines over human care. (She often reminds me that the word "tenacious" appeared in her teacher's school report when she was five years old.) Tallahassee's CEOs and executive directors alike knew well that Murdina had no qualms about reminding them where their true priorities should lie: with the suffering human being standing right in front of them.

We would often discuss the value of patience as a guiding principle in the work we were doing. Murdina was adamant that patience helped us embrace setbacks as natural—and often necessary—parts of life. As she shared her thoughts, I found myself reflecting on the physical space of Joseph House—the gardens, the vibrant colors, the art hanging on the walls—and how these elements reinforced our mission. The space itself, in all its warmth and lived-in beauty, was more than just a place to exist; it was a sanctuary that embodied the very healing we sought to nurture.

These gardens, the knockout roses, the leopard plants that a couple of years ago shot up popping yellow flowers, azaleas all bunched about and plumbagos, all shining forth glory. These plants overspilling one another as though in a hurried rush to reach to heaven's sky, appear blindingly infinite now that they belong to the earth. This is why we maintain and guard this garden as though its blossoming secured our very existence along with it. The rock pathways winding their way around the gardenias and the impatiens was shaped and formed by José who poured his life into the making of what he calls his little paradise. One of our community members, Gloria, a master gardener, guided José into the professional art of landscaping.

Amid all the beauty of these gardens remain of course all that affects the space: invasive weeds, prickly thorns, days of drought, cold winter nights. I've come to discover that just as those thrilling days of feeling the overwhelming progress gained, the growth spurts and accomplishments earned, there are changes that come, as with Joseph House itself, with calls in the middle of the night informing me that one of our brothers was arrested or is being evicted. Teilhard prays a sacred offering in his "Mass on the World" wherein we become more conscious of all that blossoms and all that diminishes, the interlacing of sorrow and hope, eliciting inside us a response to cry out that God may make all things one.

When we share in a life together, everyday moments open the possibility for God's goodness to be felt. At times it means we must sacrifice the desire for "efficiency" and "success" and simply enjoy mundane tasks together. "Go with the flow" ceases being a mere cliché and becomes a way of life.

One aspect of building this community that remains difficult is resisting how some in our community seek to import a merit system at Joseph House. Yes, there's a need for success, success as defined by their values. And understandably we all are drawn to success stories—we all are pulling for our own Seabiscuit or Rudy. But in the world of grace, meritocracies are typically toppled; they rarely survive the sheer gratuity of generosity's reign.

I have often contended with seemingly benign requests from those who aren't part of the Joseph House community that our residents do this or go to these types of meetings to meet some perceived redemption road narratives. As though there remains something they still must prove or do for us.

Of all of Jesus's radical parables, the parable of the day laborers has always struck me as the most radical of all. It's the story of how the vineyard owner employs various day laborers to work in the fields. There are those who are the first to show up, bright and early. Then as the day progresses the owner continues to enlist other laborers to work in the fields. Eventually as the sun begins setting, the day is nearly over and the owner employs a few more laborers. Well, the day ends, and it's time to settle all accounts for the day. The vineyard owner then does something scandalous. He pays everyone the same amount!

Regardless of the hour they started, they all get the same sum of money. All systems of merit are upended.

The scandal of grace—the basic operating system of God's Kingdom—is that what is given is in no way tied to, nor a function of, what was "earned." And then there's the owner's response to the workers at the end of the parable: "Think about this, why don't you?" A classic interpretive question. The parable of Jesus teaches your worth isn't a function of production, whether moral or material. The worth of the person is distinct from both the behavior of the person and their socially instrumentalized use value. "Are you envious because I am generous?" Jesus asks. Does the radicality of Jesus's generosity offend those sworn to the production-determines-worth mentality? How could it not?

When you set out to build community among those who have been incarcerated for their past behavior, it's clear that boundaries and expectations are essential for maintaining a environment. Community life, after all, demands sacrifices. There are certain aspects of life we must attend to if we wish to cultivate a healthy social dynamic. But the real danger lies in reconstructing the moral framework that ties our *value* to our *behavior*.

When I was at university, my academic advisor, David Kangas, would often remind me of the words of Kierkegaard or Spinoza, "Existence is not for any 'thing.'" Beneath the veiled mystery that anchors our being, there lies a superabundance of life—a life that carries its own inherent dignity, independent of any external judgment or desirable outcome. To truly grasp this majestic truth about ourselves, we sometimes need to pause, to hold still, and simply witness the sweetness of our own existence.

One Labor Day, a couple from the parish, John and MJ, invited me and three of my new brothers—Nathan, Jeremy, and Jason—to their beach house for a boat outing. As we swam along the shoals, we celebrated the first "free" day these brothers had known for quite some time.

Their pale, tattooed bodies melted into the glistening green sea under a perfect blue sky. That September sky seemed to fall right into the Gulf of Mexico, merging with the water, and for a moment, everything felt good. These three men—who had served close to forty years between them in Florida's prisons, much of it in solitary confinement—were now free. And there, in the vast expanse of the Gulf, John, MJ, and I bore witness to what felt like an unspoken baptism.

One of the men, holding a massive conch shell with a live snail inside, looked like he had just unearthed an ancient sea creature. The sight struck me—these men, just a month ago confined in solitary cells, were now embracing freedom with a rawness and joy that filled the air around us.

But, as life often does, that joy spilled over into something grimmer, weedier, something unforeseen.

Less than a month after we moved into our second home next door to the first, three of our new brothers fell prey to K2, a synthetic drug that, like a demon, claimed them with its explosive grip. I had met Jeremy, Nathan, and Jason in the confinement dorms of Santa Rosa. Jeremy, in fact, had been Qwan's cellmate. (It's bittersweet, knowing that some of our referrals for Joseph House come from former residents who are now incarcerated. They still feel the pull of a place like this, as haven in the storm.)

Now, though, these men were spiraling. Jason, hunched over in the front yard of our second house, arms moving like a child mimicking a boogeyman, jerky and disoriented.

I felt like I was in some zombie flick.

Not an hour later, I found Nathan, leaning against a tree in broad daylight, clutching his chest as if he could some-how steady the chaos inside him. Normally with a youthful exuberance and loquacious as Pre, now the K2 effects were devastating. Two residents, lost in the grip of a synthetic cannabis high, were unraveling before my eyes.

Shaken by the rapid descent, I rushed next door to check on Jeremy, a Haitian man from South Florida who stood confidently at about 5'4". I knew he had a long history with meth, and he had only been out of prison for four days. I knocked on his door, my heart now pounding.

"Jeremy, you in there?"

Nothing.

Then I noticed feet shadows underneath the door but no response. Finally, the door slowly opened and Jeremy stood in the doorway, teetering back and forth. Unable to speak.

I blurted out, "No Jeremy, not you too!"

Another would shortly succumb to this K2 undertow; in a matter of three hours our three most recent residents would fall to K2.

How is it possible such a great day at the water would cause them to start smoking K2? Was it a rush of energy created by unlocking a long-repressed sadness and exposing it to freedom's air? Or did such good vibes simply lead them to wanting to celebrate even more?

Sometimes our hidden life seems to conspire against us. Circumstances bring hopefulness and possibility only to be knocked off course by more powerful feelings.

"K2 flips entire prisons, bruh." Pre exclaimed as he tried to conjure the intensification of just how lethal this prison narcotic is. Pre's prognosis was bleak.

"I've seen firsthand how this spice takes down entire facilities; I mean administration, guards and inmates. K2," he added, "is the queen of prison drugs."

Now three out of five from our community were high on K2—which can be lethal at high doses. And I struggled with what to do. Should I enforce zero tolerance? Perhaps so. I'd be risking endangering the safety of the others. I was warned if I didn't make a clean sweep, meaning kicking all three out of the house, then I was enabling and putting others at risk at the house. I even caught myself wishing that Pre would just come and gather the culprits and their few belongings and drop them off at the bus station. This flight of fantasy brought me momentary relief.

Then that better version of myself broke through the daydreaming, reminding me that Nathan and Jeremy aren't broken furniture to be thrown out. But is that my enabling at work? Was I justifying inaction? These were not unfamiliar feelings. I felt the same anxious conflicted feelings before, related to gang violence, erratic behavior. Was I drawn to these dramas, and if so, why?

My sounding board in those moments was Murdina. "Now, Dustin," she'd say, "there's no one approach here; there's no one magic pill. You have to trust your instincts. I mean even though I'm not Catholic, and an old, lapsed Presbyterian, even I know you're the father here and you have to decide." Then she'd add, "I mean what's *mercy* good for if we don't actually use it in these circumstances. There's a red line to be drawn for sure, we can't welcome all the insanity into the house, but it's not a one-size-fits-all approach we're aiming for." Those were just the words I needed to take a deep breath and not panic. But then the crisis deepened.

Amid the K2 episode I called 911 when I found Nathan outside, lying in the grass, barely conscious. The paramedics came, shot him with Narcan, and took him to the hospital. "You might have saved his life tonight," said the paramedic. I understood, but all I could think that night was how miserable Jeremy and Nathan must have felt. I also felt that hot breath of concern at how this would look to our neighbors and the wider community, with ambulances coming.

When I went to the hospital, Nathan looked me in the eyes and said, simply, "I'm sorry." I could tell he felt crushed by all the K2 chaos. Nathan was familiar with the feeling of having been thrown out as he was periodically homeless starting at the age of eleven. After another difficult conversation with him, he blurted out, "Just drop me off at the dumpster." *We often grow into our childhoods,* I think to myself. This is why walking with others in their own private hells is unavoidable. But at what point does one say, I can go no further?

Both Jeremy and Nathan told me in so many words how lonely they felt. Jeremy lost both parents just in the past three years while he finished his sentence. Nathan had been down for seventeen years and often spoke of his sad childhood defined largely by drug trafficking heaped on him well before adulthood. He was easily one of the more traumatized brothers I'd accompany. I couldn't ignore these life realities while deliberating on their placement at Joseph House.

One morning during this abysmal September, I awoke to the daily besetting voices of self-doubt and the imagined voices of my harshest critics speaking in a tone of moral superiority of just how I screwed up, how I was derelict to the truth of addictions. Funny how absolute these voices sound at these times, which should clue me in that my superego is working hard to squash my effort to allow for change. This morning alongside the voice, I woke up literally singing in my head the Beatle's song, "Eleanor Rigby":

> All the lonely people
> Where do they all belong?
> All the lonely people (All the lonely people)

All three, I insisted, would have to go to detox if they wanted to stay. Two of them agreed, but Jason just walked away. I didn't want to see him go, but somewhere along the way, I'd learned that if I'm doing twice as much work for someone's recovery or reintegration as they are, I'm not helping either of us.

We held a restorative circle with Jeremy, Nathan, our staff, and myself, plus staff from a local restorative justice group. I had been struggling with how to respond to the crisis of the K2 episode. Feeling lost, I called on a few contacts at the restorative justice organization. I didn't know what to do, but I knew deep down we needed to talk—really talk—about what happened. We needed to listen, to understand why this had gone down the way it did.

In one of the early rounds, the designated circle leader posed the question, "Where are we now with the act? How do we feel about it?"

Jeremy spoke first.

"I'm not gonna lie . . . I feel goooooood," he said, grinning. "I know it sounds crazy, but I feel really happy. Like, I'm happy this all happened."

I felt my face harden. Happy? Happy about the destruction this had caused in our community? What the hell, man?

"I mean, obviously," he went on, "I'm not happy about taking drugs and hurting you all. But man, I feel love now— maybe for the first time ever. Unconditional love. You didn't just kick us out. You let us stay. That kind of love . . . I didn't think that existed. So yeah, I feel really good right now."

And in that moment, Jeremy gave us a gift. His raw authenticity transformed our collective pain into something entirely different. And in the weeks that followed, Jeremy became a leader in our community. He kept track of food deliveries, orchestrated house meetings, and even snuck off with a few plates of Thanksgiving dinner to share with people living on the streets.

One day, Pre turned to me and said, "Nathan and Jeremy are teaching us something here."

His eyes were wide, as if he had just caught a glimpse of something we had all been blind to before. "They're teaching us something about a community and sadness. Maybe even something about chaos . . . like the K2. Man, I didn't think they could come back from that demon. That demon doesn't let people go."

On the surface, the K2 fiasco felt like being swallowed by a violent undertow. Yet beneath the chaos, that same force—if met with mercy, forgiveness, and a measure of acceptance—had the potential to lead to long-term healing. That's what the K2 crisis felt like—a wave I was caught in, far beyond my control. The work of mercy, acceptance, and healing would take time and persistence. And I remain ambivalent about the best way to proceed. Wondering, as Murdina said, if truly there is no one approach, no magic pill.

Everything was a tightrope. At the same time, some community members—understandably concerned yet not fully aligned with our values—advocated for a zero-tolerance policy. I resisted that approach. It felt like a violation of a core truth I had long embraced: proximity. We can only build a true home if we remain in close relationship with those we have invited to be part of it.

But with proximity comes the need for responsibility. One of the most profound, yet often overlooked, human needs is the need for responsibility. Simone Weil touches on this in her book *The Need for Roots*, where she identifies responsibility as fundamental to human dignity. Her analysis of responsibility is for the individual to realize the part they play in the larger social organism. If one's responsibility is suppressed, especially in areas of harm, then we are saying they aren't integrally connected to the larger society. When I fail to confront the contempt I feel toward brothers who cause harm or continually cycle through the same destructive patterns, I sense I am hindering the reparative process in some way.

I decided to draft a sober living policy. Then I shared it with our community and board. When faced with calls for stricter, zero-tolerance measures, I often return to Christ's words: The Sabbath was made for man, not man for the Sabbath. A person-centered mission means keeping people at the heart of every decision, ensuring that our policies serve them—not the other way around. *Now,* I thought, *that's scripture even the lapsed Presbyterian Murdina could embrace.*

Jeremy was having to reckon his joy in his new community with this overwhelming feeling he didn't deserve these good things. "Father Dustin," he said, "I don't deserve this." I could sense in that healing night, his conflicting thoughts. I don't, Jeremy doesn't, deserve what is unexplainable: what is by its nature immeasurable. *Deserve* implies some meritocratic system. A system run amok on the shores of a kingdom built upon grace. But to arrive here requires a patience to endure what appeared before us to be hopeless. Together we talked and continued on, hunkering down into patience for a time that certainly seemed a dense fog.

Father Greg Boyle, who works among the gangs of East LA, in his book *Tattoos on the Heart,* says, "The vastness of God meets the restrictions of our humanity, words can't hold it." This love takes us out into the depths. Most of all, what I've discovered in this process of accompaniment is how reliant I am upon trusting that God is their ultimate guide and destination in these depths.

One Friday night, a few months after the K2 explosion, we gathered for a small indulgence—pizza, Häagen-Dazs ice cream, sodas—and settled in to watch boxing on Netflix. It was one of those evenings where everything aligned, opening us to a meaningful moment. We made it through the prefight banter, the hype, and the buildup. But then, slowly, one by one, we drifted off on the couches. First me, then Isaiah, and soon after, Jeremy and Sammy, all of us slipping into sleep as the main event continued to stream on the screen.

I woke up to the sound of the TV still on, the glow of the screen flickering in the dim room. I turned my head, and there was Isaiah, still asleep beside me. Our Friday night, meant to be spent in front of the fight, had transformed into an unintended slumber party.

As I looked around at the three men sleeping beside me, I couldn't help but marvel at how much had changed. Just two months ago, two of them had been locked in solitary confinement, in what the state calls the "worst of the worst": isolated, cut off, deemed beyond repair. And here we were, a small but sacred gathering, resting in the safety of each other's company. The labels, the designations, the menacing categories the state had applied to the brothers—all of it had fallen away in the quiet of that room.

We awoke, groggy and laughing, realizing that we had missed the very thing we had stayed up for. The main event. We chuckled, but in my heart, I knew the truth: we hadn't missed it. In fact, *we* were the main event.

Will these kinds of moments keep brothers from returning to prison? No. Do I think these moments will keep them sober or guarantee success in life? No. But the real point—the deeper truth—is that through the ebbs and flows, the highs and lows, love is given and received. That exchange of love is what nourishes the soul of our community. And I can't help but believe that it builds up our larger world as well.

It's a quiet revolution created in the mundane, everyday beauty of simply being with one another. And in that, we find something infinitely more enduring.

18

Home

"Hey, chaplain is on the wing," Pre's cellmate said to him. "Wait, wait no it's the Pope, the Pope! Yeah he got that white thing around his neck; it's the Pope!"

Pre said, "The Pope is in Rome, man, the Pope ain't in Milton, Florida."

But Pre wondered if this was Father Dustin, visiting after COVID. And he called out to me.

I hadn't visited any prisons since the pandemic. But in late May of 2021 a downturn in cases allowed me to schedule a visit in a brief window of opportunity quickly shut with the Delta variant.

I came around the corner toward him and saw his big smile. It felt good to be seen and welcomed. I couldn't imagine how he felt. He was soon to be released, not knowing where'd he go.

Pre was beaming. And so was I. "Pre, it is so good to see you. I had no idea I'd be seeing you here."

"Yeah," he said, "I've been asking around about you. People haven't seen you in forever."

"I know. With the pandemic and now Joseph House is up and running, things have been busy," I told him.

"Joseph House is open? Can I come?"

"It's open, Pre. We have been talking and thinking about it for a long time, but it's now open. And yes, you can come. Consider it done. We've got you."

We talked about next steps and settled on me asking Rachel, our social worker at the time, to write him to schedule a visit to discuss reentry details.

What I didn't know, what he would share only later, was how anxious he was: Would I stay true to my word? Later, he would share with a few visitors at Joseph House, "It isn't easy trusting my own heart after so many people done let me down."

But there's an inner spark to Pre, and this prison poet felt our chance meeting that day was providential.

Six months later we picked up Pre at the completion of twenty years in prison.

As we began that journey anew with Pre, he'd report to us his daily discoveries of this new world. His world went from being concrete and steel to opening into multiple worlds. His universe was expanding, especially by way of Google and YouTube, and for Pre it was intoxicating.

Walking down the aisles of Walmart one afternoon, Pre stopped in his tracks, turned to me, and said, "Damn, the freezer aisle smell." He marveled at the little things. The self-checkout aisle was another revelation for him, something that felt like magic.

One afternoon we went to the backyard shed to replenish our bird feeder, and as I opened the doors, he got a whiff of the blending scents of fertilizer and lawn mower gas fumes. You'd thought he'd just gotten a whiff of some otherworldly perfume by how bowled over in joy he was, saying, "I haven't smelled that in forever."

Going to the movie theater to see the latest *Spider Man* movie filled Pre with nostalgia because it was one of the last places he visited before being locked away for twenty years. It was as though he was simultaneously recollecting his past while also accumulating new little joys for his future.

"I know God is blessing me now," he told me, "with so many good experiences because there will be long and difficult days ahead."

Through it all, Pre felt a deep sense of belonging. He now had a place to call home and people who cared for him. It was more than just a physical space; it was a community. He was finally home, and it felt right.

Often a resident will ask me if I believe they can have their own place one day. It's a struggle, no doubt, but I assure them with patience and discipline I think it is possible. For those who've been enshackled to the monotony, tedium, violence, and the sovereign control of zero expectations that sums up prison life, it's liberating to encounter the simple pleasures that help them rebuild their world.

Watching men like Pre shake off the muck of shame and death these societal morgues heap on so many of the incarcerated has a way of lifting my eyes to higher grounds. It's like the prevailing headwinds of paradiso flow more freely every time they trust in the possibility of goodness in the future.

After eight months at Joseph House Pre moved out, settling into his new condo. Almost immediately, he began planting flowers and shrubs in his front yard. One day, I stopped by to drop off a few things for his new home. As we stood in the front yard, surrounded by his new rose bushes and a sago palm, Pre turned to me and said, "See, I'm taking a little bit of Joseph House with me."

That's what Joseph House is meant to be. We take what

we've received and plant it again, nurturing it in new soil. Others have done something similar. One of our brothers, for example, bought a replica of our living room rug and placed it in his own new home. A simple gesture, but it's meaningful. These small acts of carrying forward a piece of what we've built together show how Joseph House has taken root in our lives.

On a late January morning, Pre, Steve, and Roger (core members of our community whom I ministered to in prisons), and I went to Santa Rosa Correctional to visit men in solitary confinement. This was a historic day, because never before had a person, once warehoused in confinement at Santa Rosa, returned as a free citizen to encourage the men there.

Pre stood in the center of the wing with about eighty-five men and introduced himself. Many of the men in the wing remembered Pre from the time he was in confinement. A few former cellmates of his were there. In seconds, he was engulfed by men wanting to hear about his journey back to the free world.

Later Pre remarked to me, "Seeing those people, my brothers, my God, made my empathy come alive. I saw my face on every one of them."

That day Pre spoke, shared, and laughed with the men on the wing. And one of those men will now soon arrive to stay at Joseph House this summer. When Pre spoke with that young man in prison that day, he said, "At the finish line! You're already there; *there* is *here* already; now just stay focused. We've got you!"

To care is to wait, to allow those we accompany the space to arrive at their own resolution, to find their own way. Some believe that society's cure lies in brutal punishment, in control through suffering. But care invites a different possibility: the slow, often unpredictable process of growth and repair. It calls us to patience, to presence, to walking alongside—open not to the ease of certainty but to the unexpected ways healing can unfold.

Home is one way to create an unintrusive setting where love may emerge, where "we got you" shines out. That's why Pre often will say, "Yeah, Joseph House isn't a halfway house. It's a home."

Acknowledgments

This book, and my vocation, would not have come to be without the countless men I have met and visited in prisons, jails, Joseph House, and beyond. For their lives and their stories, I am deeply grateful.

I am profoundly thankful to Lil Coplan, my dedicated editor, whose collaborative spirit and clarity brought this challenging project to a full-fledged narrative flow. Equally, I extend my gratitude to her entire team at Orbis who helped bring the story of Joseph House to the page. I am inspired by Orbis Book's mission to publish provocative, justice-themed books in a world increasingly in need of prophetic voices. It is a humbling honor that my story is now a small part of their catalog.

I was fortunate to have found Kevin Tobin, my agent, whose willingness to listen to my story helped this book find its home at Orbis.

A few dear friends kept me grounded in this project, offering encouragement and courage when all I had were scattered notes, jumbled thoughts, and the faintest outline of a book. I am especially thankful to Sonya Cronin, who was always available to brainstorm and edit in the early more unsure stages. I am deeply grateful to Vance Sherwood, who faithfully read, edited, clarified, analyzed, and read again, transforming my project into a viable manuscript. Simply put, this manuscript would not have become a book without his dedicated accompaniment. Numerous conversations with people like Frank Pittenger, William Earnest, Maria Morrison, and Tom Neal have influenced the insights and ideas, and perhaps even the pathos, woven throughout this book. I am thankful for interlocutors like them—therapists, social workers, and theologians—all of whom have shaped this work in profound ways that they likely are unaware of.

In a time of priest shortages and increasing demands on dioceses and parishes, I feel blessed to have had Bishop William Wack as my bishop during the writing of this book as well as throughout the founding of Joseph House. His patience and willingness to dream alongside me were providential during this period of my life.

This book was not only written about a community but also because of a community. I cannot thank enough the staff and brothers at Joseph House for giving father the quiet time and space to write and reflect.

Finally, this book is about the making of a home, and for that, I am most thankful to Helen Feddon, my mom. Her enduring love and presence taught me what it means to turn a house into a true home.

Sources

Books

Alter, Robert. *The Hebrew Bible: A Translation with Commentary.* W. W. Norton & Company, 2018.

Boyle, Gregory. *Tattoos on the Heart: The Power of Boundless Compassion.* Free Press, 2010.

Boyle, Gregory. *Cherished Belonging: The Healing Power of Love in Divided Times.* Avid Reader Press/Simon & Schuster, 2024.

Derrida, Jacques. *The Death Penalty, Volume I.*, Trans. Peggy Kamuf. University of Chicago Press, 2014.

Girard, René. *The Scapegoat.* Trans. Yvonne Freccero. Johns Hopkins University Press, 1986.

Halík, Tomáš. *I Want You to Be: On the God of Love.* Trans. Gerald Turner. University of Notre Dame Press, 2016.

Hart, David Bentley. *The New Testament: A Translation.* Yale University Press, 2023.

King, Ursula, ed. *Pierre Teilhard de Chardin: Writings.* Orbis Books, 1999.

Levinas, Emmanuel. *Totality and Infinity: An Essay on Exteriority.* Trans. Alphonso Lingis. Duquesne University Press, 1969.

Main, John. *Word into Silence: A Manual for Christian Meditation.* Canterbury Press, 1991.

Metz, Johann Baptist. *Faith in History and Society: Towards a Practical Fundamental Theology.* Trans. J. Matthew Ashley. Seabury Press, 1980.

Powell, J. C. *The American Siberia; or, Fourteen Years' Experience in a Southern Convict Camp.* Homewood Publishing, 1891.

Stevenson, Bryan. *Just Mercy: A Story of Justice and Redemption.* Spiegel & Grau, 2015.

Weil, Simone. *The Need for Roots: Prelude to a Declaration of Duties Towards Mankind.* Trans. Arthur Wills. Routledge, 2002.

William of Saint-Thierry, *The Golden Epistle: A Letter to the Brethren at Mount Dieu.* Trans. Theodore Berkeley. Cistercian Publications, 1976.

Articles

Drobney, Jeffrey A. "Where Palm and Pine Are Blowing: Convict Labor in the North Florida Turpentine Industry,

1877–1923." *Florida Historical Quarterly* 72, no. 4 (1994): 411–34.

Franzen, Jonathan. "The End of the End of the Earth." *New Yorker,* May 23, 2016.

Shofner, Jerrell H. "Political Reconstruction in Florida." *Florida Historical Quarterly* 45, no. 2 (October 1966): 145–70.

Shofner, Jerrell H. "Forced Labor in the Florida Forests 1880–1950." *Journal of Forest History* 25, no. 1 (January 1981): 14–25.